SMALL ENDEARMENTS

SMALL ENDEARMENTS

NINETEENTH-CENTURY QUILTS
FOR CHILDREN AND DOLLS

SECOND EDITION
REVISED AND EXPANDED

SANDI FOX

RUTLEDGE HILL PRESS
NASHVILLE, TENNESSEE

Published in Nashville, Tennessee, by Rutledge Hill Press, Inc.
211 Seventh Avenue North, Nashville, Tennessee 37219

Typography by D&T/Bailey Typesetting, Inc., Nashville, Tennessee
Design by Harriette Bateman

Library of Congress Cataloging-in-Publication Data

Fox, Sandi.
    Small endearments : nineteenth-century quilts for children and dolls / Sandi Fox. — 2nd ed., rev. and expanded.
        p.   cm.
    Includes bibliographical references (p.   ) and index.
    ISBN 1-55853-312-5 — ISBN 1-55853-313-3 (pbk.)
    1. Children's quilts—United States—History—19th century.   2. Doll quilts—United States—History—19th century.   I. Title.
NK9112.F69   1994
746.9′7′097309034—dc20   94-11327
                                                                                                            CIP

Printed in China

1 2 3 4 5 6 7 8 — 99 98 97 96 95 94

THIS SMALL *E*NDEARMENT

IS FOR MY DAUGHTER,

*H*EATHER

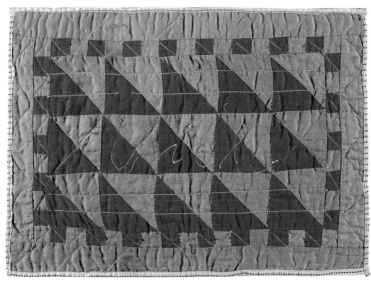

1. Machine-quilted inscription, "Viola"
Late nineteenth century
13½ x 9¾ in. (34.3 x 24.8 cm)
Collection of Muriel and David Greenberg
Courtesy of Nancy Glazer

$\mathscr{C}$ONTENTS

2. Undated stereograph
"The Quilting Bee"
Private collection

ACKNOWLEDGMENTS

A few of these small, soft links with the nineteenth century have been passed with affection from one generation to another; others have found their way by often circuitous routes into distinguished collections across the United States. Sixty-eight of those individuals and institutions now responsible for their safekeeping have allowed me to bring them together on these pages, and for their participation I am truly grateful.

There are a number of curators, collectors, and colleagues whose personal and professional generosity continues to facilitate and enhance my work. I wish particularly to thank Barbara Luck of the Abby Aldrich Rockefeller Folk Art Center, Linda Baumgarten and Carolyn Weekley of the Colonial Williamsburg Foundation, Gillian Moss of the Cooper-Hewitt Museum, Melissa Leventon of the Fine Arts Museums of San Francisco, Tod Ruhstaller of the Haggin Museum, Ann Hoenigswald of the National Gallery of Art, Alan Jutzi of the Huntington Library, Nick Thorner of the Library of Congress, Amelia Peck of the Metropolitan Museum of Art, Gerald Wertkin of the Museum of American Folk Art, Janet Fireman of the Natural History Museum of Los Angeles County, Ulysses Dietz of the Newark Museum, Celia Oliver of the Shelburne Museum, Doris Bowman of the Smithsonian Institution, and Colleen Callahan of the Valentine Museum.

For their scholarship, suggestions, and friendship, I am additionally indebted to Darwin Bearley, Linda and Irwin Berman, Gail Binney-Stiles, Robert Cargo, Tom Cuff, Nancy Druckman, Laura Fisher, Nancy Glazer, Evie Gleason, Jonathan Holstein, Glendora Hutson, Ardis and Robert James, Mary Hunt Kahlenberg, Jolie Kelter and

Michael Malcé, Rod Kiracofe, Kate and Joel Kopp, Marilyn and Ron Kowaleski, Wendy Lavitt, Rosemarie and Richard Machmer, Paul Pilgrim and Gerald Roy, Bets Ramsey, Linda Reuther, Stella Rubin, Julie Silber, Tom Woodard and Blanche Greenstein, and Shelly Zegart. The 1980 exhibition and catalogue from which this book was developed were enhanced by the participation of four treasured friends and colleagues, now gone: Edwin Binney 3rd, Robert Bishop, Phyllis Haders, and Michael Kile—I miss them all.

Much of the material on these pages is drawn from three decades of research notes, and I can only collectively thank those hundreds of librarians and archivists who have welcomed me into their reading rooms or responded to my queries.

I am fortunate indeed for the professional associations that led to this publication. With patience and persistence my agent, Rita Rosenkranz, secured a new life for an out-of-print book. Lawrence M. Stone and Ronald E. Pitkin, the guiding forces behind Rutledge Hill Press, have consistently shared and supported my expectations for a revised and expanded look at these small endearments. The manuscript has been thoughtfully edited by Amy Lyles Wilson, and Harriette Bateman has arranged with great sensitivity for the tender translation of both text and images onto the printed page.

In this thirty-fifth year of our life together, my husband John still manages to smile at the end of each of my projects and ask "What's next?" It is his affectionate sharing of both the challenge and the celebration that makes everything possible.

NOTE TO THE READER

In the middle of the 1970s, even for those of us most actively engaged in research in the field, quilt scholarship was still in its infancy. It was during this period that I was involved in my original inspection and interpretation of many of the small quilts illustrated here. All quilt scholars and historians will surely acknowledge that in light of the following twenty years of connoisseurship, what we knew then may not be what we know now. Without the opportunity for a physical reevaluation of each object, the captions in this new edition may differ from those in the original, and be less specific in detail. Dating, for example, except in certain instances, is now indicated by quarter- or half-centuries or, in even more general terms, described simply as early, middle, or late.

Except where it is called out in the text or caption or is obvious to the reader's eye, the material used in each piece is primarily tabby- or plain-weave cotton. Although the captions do not specifically indicate "doll quilt" as opposed to "child's quilt," that differentiation should be clear to the reader through text and through caption measurements. Those measurements are, because of the usually somewhat uneven nature of textile objects, approximate; they appear both in inches and centimeters, and length precedes width.

The text contains a significant amount of quoted material from primary and period sources, and grammar, punctuation, and spelling are presented as they appear in the original. Inked inscriptions and the printed material on many of the early children's handkerchiefs have faded with time and although great care was given to their transcription, many were difficult to read or were simply illegible.

SMALL ENDEARMENTS

3. Stamped in ink on the reverse of the quilt,
"Sarah Thompson"
Maryland
Mid-nineteenth century
38 x 41 in. (96.5 x 104.1 cm), including fringe
Collection of Stella Rubin Antiques, Potomac, Maryland

$\mathscr{I}$NTRODUCTION

$\mathscr{N}$ineteenth-century quilts for children and dolls are among the most fragile artifacts of our creative past, and the messages they contain are, like the objects themselves, multilayered. Worked with extraordinary aesthetic sensibilities (See illustration 3), they are the result of specific emotions, events, and labors—subtle threads that bound the quiltmaker to her work.

Faded remainders of a once rich-red pictorial toile form a wide "saver" border at the top and bottom of a plain, worn, homespun woolen blanket in a strangely supportive arrangement that assured the survival of each. The blanket was made continuingly serviceable by the addition of those pieces of fabric, and a segment of an early, unidentified toile that might otherwise have been lost found safe haven on a textile of more substantial size.

Thus preserved is an extraordinary image of childbirth (See illustration 4), a family scene caught at a moment in time when the very concept of family was in transition.[1] Indeed the family unit as such had not emerged from feudal allegiances until the seventeenth century; in the communal life of the Middle Ages, children were treated as the least of all creatures. The forces of European history began to shape the idea of family as the power of the medieval priest and lord were transferred to the father; then the smaller unit, as illustrated here, became bound together by new and personal loyalties.

The history of childhood is one of extraordinary complexity, and in eighteenth-century America rapidly changing economic, social, regional, and religious patterns made it almost impossible now for us to know how parents truly felt about their children.[2] In that century and well into the

4. Blanket (detail)
Late eighteenth-early nineteenth century
77⅞ x 64½ in. (197.8 x 163.9 cm)
*Los Angeles County Museum of Art, American Quilt
Research Center Acquisition Fund*

5. Record book (two pages)
Frederick County, Virginia
1820
*Collection of the Museum of Early Southern
Decorative Arts*

next, the dangers of childbearing and the staggering rates of infant mortality must have created in many women a climate of unvoiced fears and resentments that may have precluded powerful sentimental attachments to their children. It was only by continual childbearing that an eighteenth-century woman could fulfill her obligations to her husband and to society. In fulfillment of those expectations women married young, bore children at regular and frequent intervals, and all too often died before middle age. Their deaths were, of course, ascribed to divine will. The inscription on an eighteenth-century tombstone in Charleston, South Carolina, was not unique.

> Underneath / lies what was mortal of / Mrs. Margaret Edwards / Wife of Mr. John Edwards, Merchant of this place / Daughter of Mr. Alexander Peronneau, Gent / She Died / in Travail with her tenth Child / Aged 34 years and about 4 months / a Sincere, modest and humble Christian / . . . She committed her Soul to Him whom she ardently loved / and died without fear or a groan / Augt 27th, 1772.[3]

Two pages from a Virginia family record book (See illustration 5) confirm the continuingly fragile nature of nineteenth-century infants; Anna Hott lived barely three days, and her memorial document is further inscribed, "Ere Sin could blast, or sorrow fade/Death came with friedly care/The opening bud to Heaven convey'd/And bade it blofsom there."[4] However, by the middle of the nineteenth century, the Industrial Revolution had modified lifestyles, and better medical care had enhanced the chances of a child's survival. It was a newfound confidence in the latter that could result in the indelible inscription on a Lowell, Massachusetts, quilt (See illustrations 6 and 7):

6. Made to commemorate the birth of Alfred P. Sawyer on August 20, 1856
Lowell, Massachusetts
1856 (dated)
50 x 50 in. (127 x 127 cm), front
Collection of Rowland and Eleanor Bingham Miller

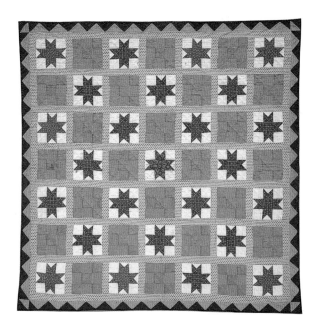

7. Reverse of Illustration 6

"Alfred P. Sawyer/Born Aug 20/1856" (See illustration 8).

Although in slowly declining numbers, children continued to die young. The bitter truths of infant mortality that were entered in ink and watercolor in those Virginia family record books and carved in stone up and down the East Coast were scratched on boards and boulders on the way to the Pacific Ocean. Seven decades after Margaret Edwards "died in travail with her tenth child" another memorial marker was worked of softer stuff. Nancy Ward Butler made this quilt (See illustration 9) to note the death of her small grandchild. It was worked full size; perhaps the extent of her sorrow could not otherwise be contained.

Although it was the responsibility of the mother to develop the child's innocence and individuality for the greater glory of the republic, the father remained a figure of unquestioned authority, but increasingly it was authority tempered with affection and concern (See illustration 10). The importance that the middle- and upper-class Victorian families placed on the sanctity of home and family existed also for those of more modest means; in this tender scene

8. Detail of Illustration 6
   Alfred P. Sawyer/Born Aug 20/1856
   Alfred P. Sawyer/Aug 20, 1856.

9. Full-size quilt
   Made by Nancy Ward Butler to commemorate
   the death of her infant granddaughter
   Jamestown, New York
   1842 (dated)
   80 x 81 in. (203.2 x 205.7 cm)
   Smithsonian Institution

10. Handkerchief

"THE HAPPY FAMILY: OR, FATHERS PRESENT"

Who took me from my mother's arms,
And smiling at her soft alarms,
Shewd me the world and natures charms,
My Father.
Who made me feel and understand,
The wonders of the sea and land,
And mark through all the Maker's hand,
My Father.
Who climb'd with me the mountains height,
And watched my look of dread delight,
While rose the glorious orb of light,
My Father.
Who from each flower and verdent stalk,
Gather'd a honey'd store of talk,
To fill the long delightful walk,
My Father.
Not on an insect would he tread,
Nor strike the stinging nettle dead,
Who taught at once my heart and head,
My Father.
Who wrote upon that heart the line,
Padia [?] grav'd on Virtue's shrine,
To make the human race divine,
My Father.
Who fir'd my breast with Homer's [illegible]
And taught the high heroic theme,
That nightly flash'd upon my dream,
My Father.
Who smiled at my supreme desire,
To see the curling smoke aspire,

From Ithaca's domestic fire,
My Father.
What made a barren rock so dear,
My boy he had a country there,
And who then dropt a precious tear,
My Father.
Upon the raft amidst the foam,
Who with Ulysses saw me roam,
His head still rais'd to look for home,
My Father.
O teach me still thy Christian plan,
Thy practice with thy precept ran,
Nor yet desert me, now a man,
My Father.
Still let the scholars heart rejoice,
With charms of thy angelic voice,
Still prompt the motive and the choice,
My Father.
Then if below while here we stay,
Along life's thorney dangerous way,
Kind heaven shall grant us while we pray,
A Father.
When death grim tyrant throws his dart
Then who powers balm into our heart,
Who then relieves the painful smart,
A Father.
For yet remains a little space,
Til I shall meet thee face to face,
And not as now in vain embrace,
My Father.
9³⁄₄ x 11⁵⁄₈ in. (24.8 x 29.5 cm)
Collection of Mary Hunt Kahlenberg, Textile Arts, Santa Fe, New Mexico

11. Thomas Faed, R. A. 1826–1900
Worn Out, 1868
Oil on canvas
41¾ x 57 in. (106 x 144.8 cm)
The FORBES Magazine Collection, New York

(See illustration 11) it is a working-class father who has thrown his common coat over the pieced quilt that has been covering his sick child and who sits with him throughout the night.[5]

In addition to those layers of sentiment and sensibilities, the surfaces of America's smallest quilts suggest an extraordinary number of stylistic sources and historical references. Through the related objects, attitudes, and interests of the nineteenth century, and through the quilts themselves, we may begin to interpret their iconography more fully. Nevertheless, as scholarly analyses contribute to our intellectual understanding of these small quilts, and subsequently to their increased significance as objects of our material culture, we must remember that these "small endearments" are objects of the heart, and therein may lie their truest worth.

NOTES

1. Ewing, plate 2. In its subject matter and in its additional detailing of bedhangings and chair, this scene is not unlike David des Granges's painting, circa 1660, of the family of Sir Richard Saltonstall, or a woodblock illustration in an 1875 Boston publication of *Rhymes for the Nursery, Mother Goose's Pocket of Pleasures*, Larkin, opp. p. 4.

2. See Beales; and Schulz, for detailed discussions of American childhood in the seventeenth and eighteenth centuries.

3. Spruill, 52.

4. Bivins, 122. For an extended discussion of a group of similarly decorated Virginia family record books, see Weekley, 1–19, in which an almost identically illustrated page, this from the Howard family book, commemorates the death of a child: "Cold is my Bed and dark the room/But Angels wait to take me home."

5. See Casteras, for additional illustrations of Victorian genre painting.

12. Christening gown and bearing cloth
England
Early eighteenth century
33 x 51¹/₂ in. (83.9 x 130.9 cm), gown
43¹/₂ x 33 in. (110.4 x 83.9 cm), bearing cloth
Los Angeles County Museum of Art, Costume Council Fund

*C*HINTZ
AND THE
EARLY YEARS

*I*n nineteenth-century America, the quilts that covered the nation's sleeping children were an exquisite condensation of the quiltmaker's craft. They were, quite simply and almost without exception, adult quilts made small through a wonderful manipulation of scale. As with their adult counterparts, the earliest of those smaller efforts were a reflection of European tastes and fashions. Few remain of those earlier elegant objects intended to comfort and clothe the eighteenth-century infant, among them an English silk quilted christening gown and bearing cloth (See illustration 12) and a child's quilt (See illustration 13) worked wholecloth from a piece of blue-resist.[1] Both in textiles and techniques, works such as these form the historical precedence for nineteenth-century quilts for American children and dolls.

The eastern seaboard had always reflect-ed its accessibility to European goods and influences, and at the end of the eighteenth century, even as America sought to establish a national identity, American women remained deliberately dependent on Europe for the most current definition of fashionable dress. French and English magazines, such as *Journal des Modes, Costumes Parisiens,* and *Gallery of Fashion,* were available through subscription or through the kindness of family or friends living abroad. Eagerly awaited letters from England or France often contained minutely detailed personal observations of the latest styles, supplemented, perhaps, with a hand-cut pattern in paper or cloth.

Once arrived on American shores, this information was transmitted to friends in other areas by similar means and with similar haste. Twenty-eight years of correspondence (1796–1824) between Margaret Manigault in Charleston and Josephine du

13. New York
Second half eighteenth century
46½ x 36½ in. (118.1 x 92.7 cm)
Colonial Williamsburg Foundation

But if fashion was about form, it was also about fabric, and it was particularly the printed and painted cottons carried into American ports that tied the American quilt-maker to European tastes. With the exception of size, the very earliest of these small endearments were more a celebration of calico and of chintz than of childhood.

The history of chintz in America, and its incorporation onto the surfaces of even the smallest of quilts and bedcovers, is a history begun in seventeenth-century England with the importation, through the East India Company, of remarkable hand-painted, mordant-dyed, and resist-printed cottons. The freshness and vitality of their designs and the vibrant colors that remained bright even after washing were the characteristics desired by fashionable London ladies. Once they had seen them, neither they nor their sisters in the colonies would do without them. Indian chintz or "calicoe" profound-ly influenced the design and manufacture of textiles for decades to come, leading eventually to the manufacture of the extra-ordinary, and primarily English, printed and painted cottons that appeared in such profusion on America's early quilts.

America's early importation of chintz can be documented through a number of printed and painted sources, from wills and watercolors to daybooks and doll quilts (See illustration 14).[4] Fortunately, the mon-etary value of early textiles merited their careful recording; household inventories of the seventeenth and eighteenth centuries, for example, list them prominently and in detail. The presence of chintz in America in the late seventeenth century is confirmed by the inventory of Margrita Visboom Van Varick, who had come from Holland to New York with her husband in 1685. Rudolphus Van Varick served as rector of the Dutch Reformed Church of Long Island

Pont in New York and Delaware chronicle their exchange of fashion plates and pat-terns: "You would certainly do well, my good Friend, to send me an organdy pat-tern of some pretty little biggin [a nightcap adopted for morning wear], if you have one."[2] Mrs. Manigault dressed a wax doll to send as a gift for little Amelia du Pont. Al-though it was surely intended to delight the child, it was equally useful as a dimension-al device by which Mrs. Manigault could transmit to Mrs. du Pont "a dress pattern which I assure you has a great deal of merit. It came to me in the latest case, and you will like it. . . . It should have three rows of lace instead of two . . . in all respects the hat is faithfully copied, and I love it madly."[3]

and at some point Margrita began to run a shop.

During the year following her husband's death in 1694, an inventory and appraisal of the contents of her own estate was taken and "the apprisement of ye Shopp goods" is rich with references to "Callico" and other textiles, and to "pinns," "thimbells," and thread ("Brown thred," "White thred," "Superfyne thred," "Courser thred").[5] Margrita's individual bequests to her children included "one stuft petticote, one Chint ditto," "two Callico quilts," "a pss of Chints and a remnent of Chints," "six callico nightgouns & two stript callico Curtins," "two callico Quilded wastcoates," "three flowerd callico petticotes," "two Cullerd callico Curtens, three smaller ditto, three Calico vallins," along with "one quilt," "one old quilt," and "one Quilt worne."[6] Of particular importance to our subject are the "Item[s] in said Basket for said Johanna & Cornelia to bee Equally devided betweene them . . . one stript cradel Cloth and one tik for a cradel bedd . . . one babyes quilt, one pin kussion . . . more thirteene callico bibbs . . . More Eight and twenty children bedds Callicos . . . forty three callico Clouts . . . six and thirty Callico pillowbears."[7] Earlier bequests included a total of eighty-three silver "childrentoyes" and "one Cradel Quilt."

Original trade documents seem to provide the richest resource for detailed references to the importation, availability, and popularity of chintz. Recorded in the Peter Jay Daybook, 1734–48, were "35 pieces of Chintz from John Isles of Bristol, consigned to John Savage and Co. merchants, Sloop Rebecca for So. Carolina."[8] Significant among such records of trade is the business correspondence of James Beekman, a successful New York dry goods dealer, contained in the *Beekman Mercantile*

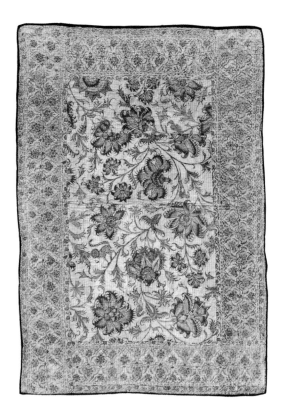

14. Probably New England
Late eighteenth or early nineteenth century
25 x 17½ in. (63.5 x 44.5 cm)
Thelma Moore Morris Collection at Jolly Mill Park

Papers. Letters to Mr. Beekman from the London firm of Pomeroy and Streatfield confirm the colonies' increasing demands for chintz:

Aug. 20, 1756
Our disappointment of an East India sale in March last which we always used to have, and out of which we were always supplied with Callicoes to print in the summer season, hath rendered it impossible to conform so regularly to Your order for quantity . . . had no chocalate ground callicoes, have sent but 13 small spots and shells instead of 24 You ordered.[9]

Those "small spots and shells" may have been similar in pattern to the designs suggested on the dresses of two women in a Pennsylvania watercolor, circa 1790 (See illustration 15), presumed to represent the harlots reveling with the Prodigal Son (Luke 15:11–32).[10] The placement of the brightly colored printed cottons on the suggestively posed ladies brings to mind the references to "Calico Madams" insultingly applied almost a century earlier to those otherwise respectable London ladies who could not be dissuaded from wearing what was, at the time, forbidden fabric. By the late 1690s, the increasing demand for imported Indian chintz had led to a commercial crisis for the English textile industry in general and for the Spittlefields silk weavers in particular. Civil disorder and parliamentary decrees having proved ineffective, the calico crisis peaked between 1719 and 1721. The weavers found themselves allied against two powerful forces: the commercial interests surrounding the East India Company and the ladies of London. Perhaps the latter seemed the tamer target, for it was against them that a remarkable series of broadsides were hurled, both literally (*The Weekly Journal*, July 4, 1719, reported the sight of the Gibbet of

15. "The Prodigal Son Reveling with Harlots"
Probably Pennsylvania, possibly Lancaster County
Possibly circa 1790
Watercolor and ink on laid paper
5^{15}/$_{16}$ x 7 in. (15.1 x 17.8 cm)
Abby Aldrich Rockefeller Folk Art Center

Stonebridge "hung from top to bottom with fragments of Callico, stuffs torn or rather stolen from Women by Journey Men Weavers") and figuratively (in songs such as those sung from broadsides in the taverns of Spittlefields.)[11] In its numerous verses, "The Weaver's Complaint Against the Callico Madames" (printed for W. Boreham in Paternoster Row, 1719) set forth the effect of the despised imports on their once-thriving industry and, consequently, on their hungry wives and children. It particularly chastised those who ignored the national, and previously flourishing, silk and wool industries, to bring home

> The Froth and The Scum
> To Dress up the Trapes like a Gay-Dame;
> And Ev'ry She Clown
> Gets a Pye-spotted Gown,
> And sets up for a Callico Madam.
> O! tawdery Callico Madam.

> [Who] neglect their own Works,
> Employ Pagans and Turks,
> And let foreign Trump'ry o'er spread em:
> Shut up their own Door,
> And starve their own Poor,
> For a tawdery Callico Madam.
> O! this Tatterdemalion Madam.[12]

In 1719, the year in which he published *Robinson Crusoe*, Daniel Defoe, the popular and respected journalist, was retained by the weavers to press their case. However, in 1726 he finally admitted that their cause was hopeless. He wrote in *A Plan of The English Commerce* that London women refused to "dress by law or clothe by Act of Parliament . . . they claim English liberty as well as the men, and as they expect to do what they please, and say what they please, so they will wear what they please, and dress how they please."[13]

Most of the patterns on the early Indian imports were either small allover motifs for personal finery or the larger designs on palampores that were meant for domestic furnishings.[14] By 1700, England, France, and Holland had mastered the Indian techniques of mordant-dyeing with madder. With the perfecting in those countries of woodblock, copperplate, and eventually roller-printing, an extraordinary diversity of design emerged. Each stylistic category was distinctive and, for clearly defined periods, fashionable. By the end of the 1700s, patterns for dress goods and for furnishing fabrics existed in extraordinary number; this is confirmed in at least two early advertisements in *Faulkner's Dublin Journal* (September 16–30, 1780, and September 12–October 19, 1782), in which English factories were being offered for sale "To Callico Printers" in Ireland "together with *200 copperplates and 2,000 Blocks and Prints,* most of which are esteemed Patterns, calculated for the general course of Foreign Trade, etc."

> The valuable and very extensive Callico-printing Plant and Implements of Thomas Nash. Esq., deceased . . . also his capital collection of upwards of *15000 wood prints, metal wax prints, and a few copper plates,* all of which are in perfect preservation; some of them are much esteemed patterns, and exceedingly well adapted for the general course of foreign and internal trade.[15]

India's glorious goods had seduced London's "Calico Madams," and by the nineteenth century their eighteenth- and nineteenth-century English offspring began to appear in increasing amounts in nineteenth-century quilts for American children and their dolls. Substantial pieces of two early textiles on the front (See illustration 16) and back (See illustration 17) of a

16. First quarter nineteenth century
45³/₄ x 42 in. (116.2 x 106.7 cm)
Collection of "All of Us Americans" Folk Art,
Bettie Mintz

17. Reverse/detail of Illustration 16

child's wholecloth quilt present stylistic characteristics suggesting both an English manufacture and a circa 1800 date. Acorns (as on the reverse) appeared during that period in a series of Richard Ovey's London patterns, including the Royal Oak and Ivy printed for him in 1799 at Bannister Hall. The late-eighteenth-century date would seem to be additionally confirmed because of the textile composing the quilt's surface and the presence of honeycombed and dotted leaves within the popular, floral-striped format. However, a striped pattern of similar honeycombed leaves (coincidentally including acorns in its alternating stripes) is presumed to have been printed in America by Archibald Hamilton Rowan, who was briefly (1797–99) engaged in textile printing at Barley Mill on the Brandywine River

near Wilmington, Delaware. A piece of that textile is in the collection of the Historical Society of Delaware, and the corresponding pattern appears twice in Rowan's pattern book.[16] Rowan is considered to have drawn heavily on contemporary English designs, as did John Hewson.

Even the smallest of American quilts (See illustration 18) have in many instances become invaluable repositories for the last segments, often unidentified, of the early English printed cottons that were produced in such extraordinary numbers.[17] An exceptionally early doll's quilt (See illustration 19) worked for a four-poster bed has as the motif for its center medallion a sailing vessel in a vignette cut from an English block print, done in Pompeian colors, circa 1805. The selvedges of the textile (See il-

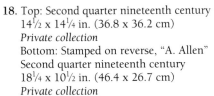

19. New England
First quarter nineteenth century
18³/₄ x 17¹/₂ in. (47.6 x 44.5 cm)
Collection of Stella Rubin Antiques, Potomac, Maryland

18. Top: Second quarter nineteenth century
14¹/₂ x 14¹/₄ in. (36.8 x 36.2 cm)
Private collection
Bottom: Stamped on reverse, "A. Allen"
Second quarter nineteenth century
18¹/₄ x 10¹/₂ in. (46.4 x 26.7 cm)
Private collection

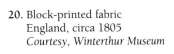

20. Block-printed fabric
England, circa 1805
Courtesy, Winterthur Museum

lustration 20) from which it was taken contain the three blue threads required between 1774 and 1811 on all cotton cloth of English manufacture, thus confirming the textile's origin and early date. The small squares that surround the ship are precious cargo indeed; all seem to have been printed before 1820 and many of them may well be the last bit of their original, larger, printed selves.

If small floral prints were more desirable for ladies' dresses, it was more often the larger motifs found on furnishing fabrics that dressed their homes, and they too found their way onto the quilts worked for their children. A substantial segment of a French copperplate-printed textile, Les Asphodel, forms the central panel, one small square, and five of the larger triangles pieced into the surrounding borders of a

21. First quarter nineteenth century
46 x 41 in. (116.8 x 104.1 cm), front
Collection of Robert B. Haas and Mariko Hibbett

22. Reverse of Illustration 21

23. Reverse/detail of Illustration 21

24. "African Hospitality"
   Gravure en mezzo teinte publiée á Londres en
   Fév.
   1791 par Smith-King Street Covengarden.
   D'aprés le tableau de G. Morland.
   Collection H. D'Allemagne
   *LA TOILE IMPRIMEE ET LE INDIENNES DE
   TRAITE*

Henry-René D'Allemagne
Noties par Henri Clouzot
Tome 1
Paris, Librairie Grund, MCMXL 111
NK 8809 A4 V. 1
*Courtesy Library, Cooper-Hewitt, National
Museum of Design, Smithsonian Institution/Art
Resource, NY*

child's quilt (See illustration 21) in a surface arrangement suggesting the English preferences of the period for a central medallion.

Copperplate pictorials, circa 1760–90, and their roller-printed descendants, were often worked as wholecloth quilts for adult beds, often forming the bedhangings as well; on occasion a piece appears (usually as the backing fabric) on a child's quilt, a remnant perhaps from that larger project. The textile on the reverse (See illustration 22) of the Les Asphodel quilt is an example of the legacy of those eighteenth-century monochromatic renderings that drew upon illustrations from literary, historical, biblical, and other written sources.[18] The dramatic scenes on these panels correspond in several instances to those found on other surfaces. One of the faded blue tableaux (See illustration 23), set here beneath lush palm trees, is the image of another isolated group at the sea's rough edge that is the subject of a 1791 print, "African Hospitality" (See illustration 24).[19] The same image, reversed and with altered background (See illustration 25), appears on another textile with several other scenes that are identical to those on the child's quilt; here the fabric formed a bed curtain (See illustration 26). In both textiles the scenes appear to illustrate the slave trade. It is confirmed on the latter, Traite des Négres, but the original literary source for these illustrations has not been substantiated. Many elements, particularly in this single selected image, suggest *The History of Paul and Virginia: or the Shipwreck* (1787), set on an island in the Indian Ocean. Paul eventually awaits the return from France of his beloved Virginia. The description of the storm and of the shipwreck just off the island, in which she perishes, is not unlike that depicted on the etching and textiles. The illustration of a

25. Furnishing fabric
Traite des Négres
France, 1790–1805
67¾ x 33 in. (172.1 x 83.8 cm), detail
Los Angeles County Museum of Art, gift of Mrs. Henry Salvatori

26. Full repeat of Illustration 25

man and dog might refer to Paul, with his dog Fidele, being comforted by his slave, Domingo. We know of at least one school-girl embroidery on which these characters appeared, worked by Sarah Forster in Massachusetts, circa 1810, and now a part of the Abby Aldrich Rockefeller Folk Art Collection.[20]

Another pictorial, this printed in red, forms the reverse (See illustration 27) of another small quilt (See illustration 37). Although the source of these illustrations is also unidentified, the scenes suggest those of a popular novel. The textile itself can be confidently placed within a group dating from about 1820. As a less expensive substitute for the rich, copperplate-printed pictorials of the previous century, these were printed from metal rollers.[21]

The substantial number of surviving

27. Second quarter nineteenth century
35½ x 35½ in. (90.2 x 90.2 cm), reverse, detail
Private collection

full-size quilts and bedhangings (or segments thereof) constructed from these pictorial furnishing fabrics suggest their popularity and wide use. In Massachusetts, Lucy Larcom remembered:

> There was on my mother's bed a covering of pink chintz, pictured all over with the figure of a man sitting on a cloud, holding a bunch of keys. I put the two together in my mind, imagining the chintz counterpane to be an illustration of the poem, or the poem an explanation of the Counter-

pane . . . "St. Peter sat at the celestial gate, / And nodded o'er his keys."[22]

From 1760 to 1790, copperplate-printed textiles overshadowed the block-printing techniques that had been established in England by the 1680s. But for block-printed textiles for furnishing and dress fabrics, 1790 was the beginning of a truly golden age. Working with patterns, written records, and textile fragments from the following two decades, Peter Floud and Barbara Morris

28. Block-printed fabric
England, circa 1780
Plain-weave cotton
Repeat height: 84.5 cm
Purchase in memory of Mrs. John Innes
Kane (1953-19-3)
Courtesy Cooper-Hewitt, National Museum of Design, Smithsonian Institution/Art Resource, NY

29. Detail of Illustration 28

published a series of scholarly articles during the late 1950s that established the stylistic progression of chintz design between 1790 and 1810. These articles remain definitive in the field, establishing periods of popularity as narrow as three to five years. All of those textiles, and related patterns roller-printed after 1810, also found great popularity in the United States, many making their way in smallest measure onto quilts for children and dolls.

On the arborescent chintz that appeared in the latter part of the eighteenth century, gnarled and undulating branches were laden with exotic blooms, both stylized and naturalistic, and often playing host to a variety of brightly plumed birds. Those textiles proved to be particularly fertile fields for the selection of motifs that would soon embellish the most elegant of early American quilts. Perhaps none was more prominent than a textile (See illustration 28) block-printed circa 1780, whose huge, menacing birds and several smaller birds and floral motifs appear on a remarkable number of very early full-size quilts and bedcovers. Almost half a century after its original manufacture, and coupled with more common cloth, segments of that textile (See illustration 29) were worked onto the surface of a small Maryland quilt (See illustration 30), providing a unique opportunity to illustrate *broderie perse,* a technique in which motifs are cut from chintz and appliquéd onto a solid ground.[23] The birds that perch on slender stalks, feeding delicately on berries and leaves, were cut

from at least two repeats of fabric printed an ocean, and almost a half-century, away, as were the floral sprays placed in the corners and the segments of branches appearing in the appliquéd basket.

It was probably an arborescent chintz observed by little Laura Russell (born 1827) in the home of her "dame":

30. Carroll County, Maryland
Second quarter nineteenth century
43¼ x 34¾ in. (109.9 x 88.3 cm)
Collection of Gail Binney-Stiles

31. Block-printed fabric
Produced by Bannister Hall Printworks
Lancashire, England, 1815
Plain-weave cotton
Offset repeat height: 41.25 cm
Gift of Clifton S. Billings (1971-79-2)
Courtesy Cooper-Hewitt, National Museum of
Design, Smithsonian Institution/Art Resource, NY

It was simply a low bedstead with hinges at the head, the bed and bedding being tied down to keep them in place and the whole turned up against the wainscot during the day, a curtain which hung from ceiling to floor concealing it. The curtain was of highly glazed chintz suspended from a projecting frame and adorned with impossible birds, trees and flowers of the most gaudy colors. It was the only work of art which the room contained and we were never tired of gazing upon its splendors.[24]

It was not only little girls such as Lucy Larcom and Laura Russell who had recorded in their mind's eye the pleasure of the bright chintz that hung in those early bedrooms. William Nowlin remembered his mother's bed in their bark-covered home in the Michigan woods: "On the foot and front of the frame were pinned calico curtains with roses and rosebuds and little birds, some perched on a green vine that ran through the print, others on the wing, flying to and from their straw colored nests."[25] Certainly the pleasure would have been doubled had several of those vivid images been transferred to their own childhood quilts.

Palm trees and game birds (See illustration 31) were printed in multiple variations: pheasants and quail and strange crested birds with exotic trees and flowers, often in white-rimmed islands of color (See illustration 203, "For the Dolls"). These textiles appeared in significant numbers as wholecloth quilts and provided convenient cut-outs to place in corners or elsewhere as supporting motifs, both on small quilts (See illustrations 32 and 33) and on large ones. They often surrounded (as they do here) the similarly popular motif of a flower-filled vase, itself having perhaps been drawn from the last remaining piece

32. Second quarter nineteenth century
34 x 30 in. (86.4 x 76.2 cm)
*The Baltimore Museum of Art, gift of Linda
and Irwin Berman, St. Simons Island,
Georgia
Photograph courtesy of America Hurrah
Antiques, NYC*

33. Second quarter nineteenth century
68 x 64 in. (172.7 x 162.6 cm)
Ex Binney collection

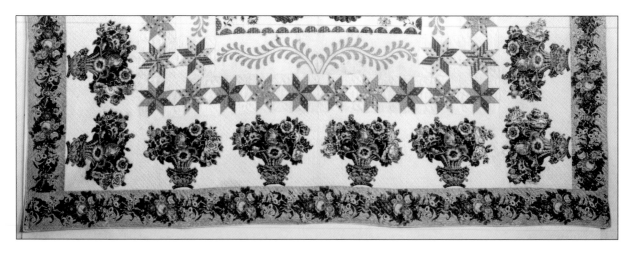

34. Full-size quilt
Second quarter nineteenth century
108½ x 106½ in. (275.6 x 270.5 cm), detail
Copyright © Sotheby's, Inc.

of a textile that had provided cut-out elements for the extravagant border of a full-size quilt (See illustration 34).

The first application of classical design to the usually exclusively floral block-printed chintz came with the introduction of the pillar print in the last decade of the eighteenth century, an extravagantly embellished column (See illustration 35), usually Ionic or Corinthian. The long-reaching textile pillars proved an ideal motif for furnishing fabrics in rooms with high ceilings, for wholecloth quilts and bedhangings, and for the wide strips that so often formed the border for elegant pieced or appliquéd quilts, large and small (See illustration 36).

Two children's quilts (See illustrations 37 and 38) contain between them a number of these English cottons. In addition to its pictorial backing (See illustration 27), the border of the first and more fragile one holds a very early pillar print, cut crossgrain. The fabrics in the central field of the second include a number of early printed

35. Roller-printed fabric
England, 1825–35
Plain-weave cotton
Repeat height: 34/3 cm
Gift of Mrs. Ralph P. Hanes (1978-167-3)
Courtesy Cooper-Hewitt, National Museum of Design, Smithsonian Institution/Art Resource, NY

36. Mid-nineteenth century
50 x 40 in. (127 x 101.6 cm)
Collection of Fleur Bresler
Courtesy of Stella Rubin

37. Second quarter nineteenth century
$35\frac{1}{2}$ x $35\frac{1}{2}$ (90.2 x 90.2 cm)
Private collection

38. Second quarter nineteenth century
$50\frac{1}{2}$ x $48\frac{1}{4}$ in. (128.3 x 122.6 cm)
Collection of Myra Aronson

39. Second quarter nineteenth century
  5³⁄₈ x 5 in. (13.7 x 12.7 cm), front
  Private collection

40. Second quarter nineteenth century
  5³⁄₈ x 5 in. (13.7 x 12.7 cm), reverse
  Private collection

and painted cottons, including examples of dark ground chintz, and many retain their original glaze. Both pieces are constructed in the English pieced-paper method that for many American quiltmakers remained the method of choice for piecing hexagons (See illustrations 39 and 40) throughout the nineteenth century. Often it was also used for other geometric shapes, particularly those worked in silk:

> Rich materials look very handsome in mosaic patterns. . . . Old envelopes, or other waste writing-paper . . . may be

used in backing up the pieces. The . . . material is then tacked onto the paper and various pieces are sewn together. It requires care to arrange the colours well. The study of any mosaic woodwork will greatly aid in this, as far as the effects of light and shade are concerned.[26]

Particular attention was paid to the method by which the quilt would be bound. Elaborate edgings, frequently drawn from elements and embellishments on costume of the period, were often applied to these small pieces: tape binding (See illustration 27), English or American manufactured, or handwoven on a tape loom (See illustration 41); tiny piping such as the bit of blue that defines the limits of an early cotton Starburst (See illustration 42); and elaborate fringes that were tatted, crocheted, and knotted, both commercially and by hand (See illustration 43).

These, then, were among the earliest quilts for America's children and dolls (See illustration 44). Within her separate sphere, society required a woman to ensure her children's sleep, to keep them safe and warm; it was the inclination of the quilt-maker's heart and hands that they should sleep in beauty. It was out of the sentimental attachments society now encouraged that these small endearments evolved—a fulfillment of society's dictates and sentiment's designs.

41. Tape loom
Carved inscription "D W 1814"
Oak base with hickory and maple turned members
18 x 30$\frac{1}{2}$ in. (45.7 x 77.5 cm)
Collection of the Museum of Early Southern Decorative Arts

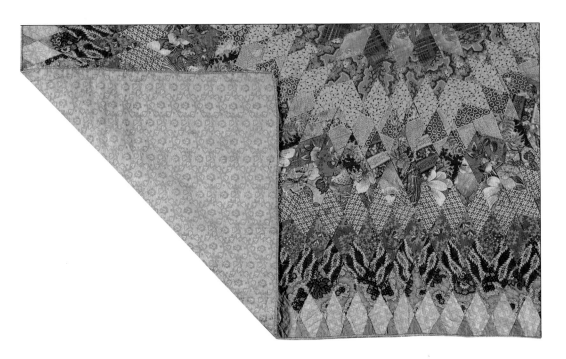

42. Second quarter nineteenth century
41$\frac{1}{2}$ x 38$\frac{3}{4}$ in. (105.4 x 98.4 cm), detail
Private collection

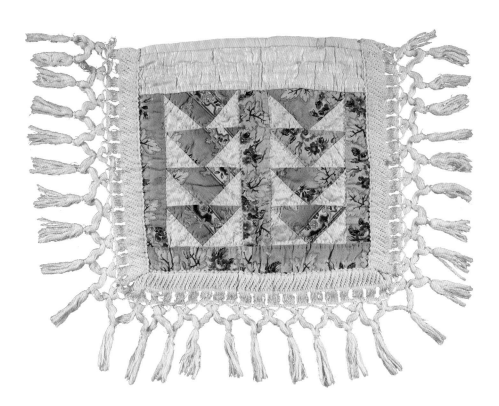

43. First quarter nineteenth century
11½ x 15½ in. (29.2 x 39.4 cm), including
fringe
Collection of Nancy Glazer

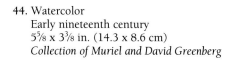

44. Watercolor
Early nineteenth century
5⅝ x 3⅜ in. (14.3 x 8.6 cm)
Collection of Muriel and David Greenberg

NOTES

1. The christening gown and bearing cloth were shown in a 1988 exhibition curated by the author, "To Comfort and Clothe: Quilts and Quilted Clothing from the Permanent Collection 1700–1860" at the Los Angeles County Museum of Art. The exhibition also included a pair of full-size quilts constructed from two different and distinctive blue-resist patterns, one a pheasant amid foliage and the other (illustrated in Fox, *Quilts,* no. 9) a parrotlike bird on a vertical floral vine. These two quilts descended through the family of one of the original settlers of Greenwich, Connecticut, and the child's quilt (See illustration 13) is thought to have come from the van Rensselaer family in upper New York (Pettit, *Printed and Painted Fabrics,* 141), placing both within the only areas in which these elusive textiles have appeared: the Hudson River Valley, Western Connecticut, and on Long Island. All three belong to a group of indigo resist-printed fabrics whose point of manufacture is still in doubt. The author remains unaware of any example having been found in England, and Peter Floud (the late curator of London's Victoria and Albert Museum) determined them to be American (Pettit, *Printed and Painted Fabrics,* 141), yet a 1766 British excise stamp appears on the reverse of a related blue-resist owned by the Albany Institute of History and Art, New York (illustrated in F. Montgomery, *Printed Textiles,* fig. 187). For further illustrations and information on designs and technique, see F. Montgomery, 194–211; and Pettit, *Indigo Blues.*

2. Low 1974, 57. Mrs. Managault to Mrs. du Pont (in French), Charleston, 6 April 1800.

3. Ibid., 74. Mrs. Managault to Mrs. du Pont (in French), Charleston, 24 December 1800. The extent of the fashionable details conveyed by this doll is suggested by a 29 December addendum to the letter accompanying Amelia's gift: "Besides the doll and that hat there is a band. You will readily see that the corner makes the fichu, that it is attached with a pin, that the two small knots are found on the shoulders. But instead of the little gold pin that holds the crossed ribbon, a buckle or a gold ornament is needed. You surely have one. And then after crossing it on the chest, it is knotted in the back. The little veil on the hat can be worn over the eyes or else lifted up as it is, and that is the way I like it." For additional information on early dressed dolls, see Baumgarten 1991.

4. Tiny fantastic creatures and small exotic birds sometimes appear on the early Indian palampores, almost hidden in branches and hillocks, and they appear on the very early chintz that forms the central field of this faux-palampore doll quilt.

5. Montgomery, C., 1962b, 1–5.

6. Montgomery, C., 1962a, 4–6.

7. Ibid., 5. The "pin Kussion" to which this bequest refers is probably a layette pincushion. As a discreet display of the economic status suggested by an ample supply of pins, it was fashionable during that century and the next to work a layette pincushion for a newborn on which a message was spelled out in that precious commodity (although manikin or "dummy" pins were often used).

In her Diary, 12, (December 30, 1771), Anna Green Winslow noted: "My aunt stuck a white sattan pincushion for Mrs. Waters. On one side, is a plathorn with flowers, on the reverse, just under the border are, on one side stuck these words, Josiah Waters, then follows on the end Decr. 1771, on the next side & end are the words Welcome Little Stranger." Although these "sticking" pincushions marked other occasions and celebrations, that poignant phrase, "Welcome Little Stranger," may have been stuck more than any other, either alone or in variation.

According to Andere, 67, during the siege of Boston, a baby was given a pincushion that read, "Welcome, little stranger, Though the port is closed." In the early nineteenth century, another carried the message, "God assist the mother through her danger, And protect the little stranger."

8. Beer, 37.

9. Beekman, 630–635. A descriptive term *shells,* as used in this letter, illustrates a common problem in our contemporary interpretation of period terminology. Sea shells did indeed appear

in realistic, if romantic, form on early textiles, but this 1756 usage would describe a repeating pattern of small sprigged flowers as illustrated in F. Montgomery, *Printed Textiles*, fig. 75. Later, on a roller-printed textile, circa 1825–35, illustrated in F. Montgomery, *Printed Textiles*, fig. 247, sea shells in sepia tones appear with coral and seaweed. The selected images corresponded with a period in which Lucy Larcom remembered that in her early New England village "Mantel-pieces were adorned with nautilus and conch-shells, and branches and fans of coral," (Larcom, *Girlhood*, 94.)

10. Abby Aldrich Rockefeller Center, 247.

11. Plummer, 296.

12. Ibid., 297.

13. Ibid., 306.

14. See Beer, 47–123, for extensive illustration of those palampores in the contained catalog of the collection of Indian chintz at the Cooper-Hewitt Museum in New York City; and Irwin and Brett for relevant objects in the collections of the Royal Ontario Museum in Toronto and the Victoria and Albert Museum in London.

15. Longfield, 72. Longfield points out the difficulty in establishing the point of manufacture of any textiles printed from those copperplates and woodblocks if they were indeed purchased by an Irish "callico printer."

16. The textile is illustrated in Pettit *Printed and Painted Fabrics*, fig. 127, and the pattern is illustrated (with extensive text on Rowan) in F. Montgomery, *Printed Textiles*, 98–103.

17. In their series of articles in *The Connoisseur* (1957–1959), Peter Floud, then keeper of circulation in the Victoria and Albert Museum, and his colleague, Barbara Morris, then senior research assistant in that museum, presented conclusions drawn from research based on records of various textile printers that had only recently been made available to them for comparison and study. The articles frequently note that no piece of actual fabric from a particular pattern had been found. But the fabrics may remain, unnoticed, in the quilted documents that are America's quilts. The author particularly recommends to the reader Callahan, 97–140, for an exemplary analysis of a pieced quilt (1795–1805) in the collection of the Metropolitan Museum of Art, in the small pieces of which Colleen Callahan identifies thirty-seven individual printed designs: nine copperplate-printed, twenty-eight woodblock-printed, and fragments from five woodblock-printed bird designs and many woodblock-printed floral designs.

18. Two plays and two travel books, for example, were the source of design for four English copperplate-printed textiles in the collection at Colonial Williamsburg. See Cox for illustrations and discussion.

19. D'Allemange MCMXL 111, plate XV.

20. The etching of "The corpse of Virginia discovered upon the beach" that prefaced the 1802 English translation shows Paul and Domingo making the tragic discovery. See Pitoiset, 111, illustration, an 1800 textile, "Paul et Virginie," and an 1810 toile de jouy showing Paul grieving alone.

21. Floud, *Pictorial Prints*, 456–459.

22. Larcom, 130. The chintz to which Lucy refers may be an 1820 toile illustrated in Pitoiset, fig. 231.

23. For a technical description of this method see Fox, *Wrapped in Glory*, 26.

24. Russell, 20.

25. Nowlin, 115. He may be referring to one of the English roller-printed textiles taken from, or inspired by, Audubon's *Birds of America*. See also Morris, *Designs*, 560–563.

26. Hamilton, 321.

A COMMON VOCABULARY:

THE DECORATIVE ARTS

*A*merican quiltmakers shared with other craftsmen and artisans of the period a rich and extensive vocabulary of design, perhaps nowhere more apparent than in the rendering of a lattice basket (See illustration 45). These were not the baskets to be filled and emptied and refilled in the endless repetition of "woman's work," holding bits of plain sewing, feathers, or vegetables from her garden. These were gloriously embellished, overflowing with flowers, foliage, and fruit, and as such they became a common design throughout America's decorative arts.

The motif appeared early: worked in silver or on elegant china and common clay; carved in wood by Samuel McIntire onto a Salem, Massachusetts, mantelpiece; worked in watercolor (See illustration 46) and in pencil and ink; stenciled on velvet on schoolgirl theorems. It appeared printed on textiles (See illustration 35, "Chintz and the Early Years") that were in turn used on quilt borders or used wholecloth as a backing (See illustration 47). As the central motif on nineteenth-century quilts for children, the lattice basket was worked in all the most sophisticated techniques of the craft: in quilting and stuffed work (See illustration 48) on an ambitious piece worked in New England in the first quarter of the century; in *broderie perse* (See illustration 49), its surface arrangement of a two-handled basket surrounded with floral borders similar to a composition on a stenciled textile (See illustration 50) of indeterminate function that bears, beneath its basket, the faded imprint of a metal stamp such as those used on friendship or presentation quilts and containing two sets of illegible initials; and filled and bordered with appliquéd leaves, roses, and buds (See

45. "Easter Rabbit"
Late eighteenth century
Watercolor and ink on laid paper
3³/₁₆ x 3³/₁₆ in. (8.1 x 8.1 cm)
Abby Aldrich Rockefeller Folk Art Center

46. Theorem painting
American School, circa 1825
Watercolor, pen and ink on paper
11³/₄ x 16 in. (30 x 41 cm)
Copyright © Sotheby's, Inc.

47. Reverse of child's quilt, circa 1840, detail
Ex collection Marilyn and Ron Kowaleski

48. First quarter nineteenth century
39 x 40 in. (99.1 x 101.6 cm), including netted
fringe
Private collection
Photograph courtesy of America Hurrah Antiques,
NYC

illustration 51), the flowers layered and
embellished with embroidered stitches, all
on a butternut-dyed ground and inscribed
in ink beneath the basket, "Presented to
Mrs. Margaret M. C[illegible] by her mother."

The lattice basket appears also on a
splendidly embroidered child's quilt (See illustration 52), one that presents an example of the difficulty of differentiating between origins and influences. The basket
and its surrounding border are finely and
imaginatively worked in a great variety of
embroidery stitches, as are the four corner
blocks that contain its wholecloth borders.
A cross-stitched inscription, "M M– / June
27th– / 1844" (See illustration 53) is again
entered beneath the basket. As a binding,

49. First quarter nineteenth century
41 x 40 in. (104.1 x 101.6 cm)
The Baltimore Museum of Art, gift of Linda and
Irwin Berman, St. Simons Island, Georgia
Photograph courtesy of Thos. K. Woodard
American Antiques & Quilts

50. Stenciled textile
Attached note: "Janet S. Smith & F. Rand,
Tunbridge."
Tunbridge, Vermont
Second quarter nineteenth century
30 x 31 in. (76.2 x 80 cm)
Courtesy of Frank and Barbara Pollack American
Antiques & Art, Highland Park, Illinois

fabric from the reverse of the quilt has been folded over the quilt's edge, and the piece may in fact have been the central section cut from a worn or damaged full-size quilt. Wear on the turned binding and other supporting evidence indicates, however, that if this is the case it was probably done in the nineteenth century.[1] The stylistic characteristics of this piece, a central medallion of embroidered lattice basket and floral border then surrounded by a wide wholecloth border of a striped fabric cut cross-grain, are identical to several full-size quilts of Irish origin, including one in the collection of the Ulster Folk and Transport Museum. Beneath that basket is inscribed, in cross-stitch, "Roseanna Butler 17 August 1844 Randalstown, Co. Antrim."

51. Inscribed in ink beneath the basket, "Presented to Mrs. Margaret C[illegible] by her mother" Mid-nineteenth century
41¼ x 44 in. (104.8 x 111.8 cm)
Los Angeles County Museum of Art, gift of Ann Ziol

52. Cross-stitched inscription, "M M–/June 27–1844–"
American or Irish
1844 (dated)
36¼ x 37 in. (92.1 x 94 cm)
Los Angeles County Museum of Art, American Quilt Research Center Acquisition Fund

In the middle of the nineteenth century, in Baltimore and its surrounding area, the art of appliqué had come to full and formal flower on a remarkable group of quilts that have come to be known collectively as Baltimore Album quilts. They form a unique body of work characterized by remarkable consistencies in design and execution. Perhaps only this one example (See illustration 54) remains of its most classic form reduced for a child, the small fruit of those larger cultural and creative labors. This piece was made for Mary Emig, born in Emigsville, Pennsylvania; it may have been worked by Baltimore kin or as the result of a visit to, or a visitor from, that more sophisticated city. The turnpike between Baltimore and Pennsylvania that carried the goods of commerce could also have carried this small quilt or, perhaps, its thoughtful beginnings. Epergnes and cornucopias are filled with flowers in stylized compositions; multiblossomed branches are worked in both open and closed wreaths in neoclassical ornamentation, and in sprays both crossed and tied. The decorative motifs on little Mary's quilt are those of the full-size Baltimore Album quilts and of craftsmen working in other materials in Baltimore and elsewhere. The lyre, for example, was also found on Duncan Phyfe's New York chairs and on the footpedal support of a concert grand piano made in Boston by Jonas Chickering.

53. Detail of Illustration 52

Two specific elements from the larger Baltimore quilts appear on this smaller piece: sections of reverse appliqué used on identical tulips and several flowers and basket handles formed of overlapping "coins" of fabric. The popular rainbow or "fondu" prints (single-color fabrics with a gradual intensity of shading), so effectively employed on the larger pieces are not present, but the border print strengthens the creative connection. Looking closely at the deteriorated segments that cling stubbornly to the cotton batting, one can still discern the red, gold, and black colors, and the faint shapes of the acanthus scrolls and leaves that were used in the French Restoration-style fabrics. The acanthus fabric on this small quilt is similar, if not identical, to the border fabric and certain appliquéd motifs used occasionally on full-size Baltimore Album quilts.[2]

There is one classic motif missing from this quilt that is often found on the most distinguished of the larger Baltimore quilts, that of a great blue eagle, its wings and tail feathers embellished with teardrop shapes of yellow, holding in its beak a ribbon-tied floral spray and grasping in its talons two poles that hold a liberty cap and the nation's flag. The design would be difficult to execute on a smaller block, and indeed one single unit, worked originally for inclusion on a larger quilt, has been extensively trimmed to become the one touch of elegance on a simpler child's quilt (See illustration 55).

The requirements for a symbol are that it appear in great profusion in a number of media and that its meaning be clear and continuing. Although Benjamin Franklin considered the eagle to be "a bird of bad moral character" and Nathaniel Hawthorne, observing the great carved eagle at the Salem Custom House, noted "the customary infirmity of temperament that characterizes this unhappy fowl,"[3] its selection by the Continental Congress as our national symbol and its placement on the Great Seal of the United States was generally celebrated as a grand and inspired choice. Its image was soon everywhere within sight of young and impressionable eyes, worked by craftsmen in every field: carved and molded, embroidered and incised; printed and painted; and stamped, stenciled, and sewn. An English textile, "Eagle and Shield from Seal of the United States," circa 1825, was printed for the American market and the significant amounts that appear in extant examples of quilts (See illustration 56) and bedhangings suggest its popular reception. The period assigned to a nationalistic fervor for this image in American design is generally considered to be approximately 1790–1840.[4] It continued, however, as an important motif on American quilts, many

55. Mid-nineteenth century
50 x 36 in. (127 x 91.4 cm)
Private collection

54. Made for Mary Emig
Emigsville, Pennsylvania
1847
58½ x 44¾ in. (148.6 x 113.7 cm), including fringe
Los Angeles County Museum of Art, gift in honor of Sara Marie Habib

on those Baltimore quilts worked for personal rather than patriotic purposes: on a quilt made by his friends for Benjamin Foard of Folk, Baltimore County; on a bride's quilt made for Miss Isabella Batty on the occasion of her marriage to Mr. Andrew Crow, October 12, 1852; on a freedom quilt given to Benjamin Almoney in 1845 on his twenty-first birthday; and on a quilt worked in 1843 by Sophia Bankard Whitaker for her own pleasure.[5]

There were other motifs on these small

quilts, held in common with all those who labored to make the functional also beautiful, such as the Pineapple (See illustrations 57 and 58), the Laurel Leaves (See illustration 59), the Prince's Feather (See illustrations 60 and 61).

That which embellished the quiltmaker's home was consistently adapted to the surfaces of her dearest quilts, and the heavily draped and tasseled curtains (See illustrations 62 and 63) at her mid-nineteenth-century windows may have suggested the swag and tassel borders on the quilts on her children's beds (See illustration 64).[6]

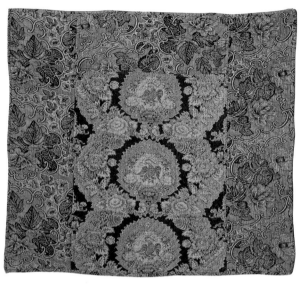

56. Second quarter nineteenth century
37 x 42¼ in. (94 x 107.3 cm)
The Baltimore Museum of Art, gift of Dena S. Katzenberg

57. Made by Rachel Smith of Derby, Connecticut, while visiting her grandniece, Mrs. John B. Morris, in Newark, New Jersey
Third quarter nineteenth century
59 x 38½ in. (149.9 x 97.8 cm), detail
Collection of The Newark Museum, gift of Mary Elizabeth Morris and John B. Morris, Jr., 1935

58. Inscribed in ink, "Sallie J. Davault"
Fourth quarter nineteenth century
19½ x 21¼ in. (49.5 x 54 cm)
Collection of Jonathan and Gail van der Hoof

59. Attributed to Mrs. L. G. Richardson
Woburn, Massachusetts
Mid-nineteenth century
40 x 40 in. (101.6 x 101.6 cm)
Collection of Glendora Hutson

60. Fourth quarter nineteenth century
37 x 36½ in. (94 x 92.7 cm)
Los Angeles County Museum of Art, gift of Felicia Melero Holtzinger

62. Prior Hamblen School
Courtesy of Frank and Barbara Pollack American Antiques & Art, Highland Park, Illinois

61. Pennsylvania
Last quarter nineteenth century
49¼ x 47 in. (125.1 x 119.4 cm)
Collection of Herb Wallerstein

63. Prior Hamblen School
Courtesy of Frank and Barbara Pollack American Antiques & Art, Highland Park, Illinois

64. Third quarter nineteenth century
37½ x 36½ in. (95.3 x 92.7 cm)
Ex collection Phyllis Haders

NOTES

1. A similar example (illustrated in Fox, *Small Endearments,* 1980, 150) is suggested by a tape-bound piece (circa 1800) formerly in the collection of the Winterthur Museum, in which an embroidered panel with flower-filled urn and scattered floral motifs may have been cut down from a larger and earlier piece possibly worked in the eighteenth century. The relaxed lines and open spaces on this early piece suggest the embroidery to be American rather than English Jacobean embroidery, which is characterized by a rigid formality and heavily worked backgrounds.

2. See illustration in Fox, *Wrapped in Glory,* 69.

3. Hawthorne, 7–8.

4. Fleming, 283.

5. Dunton, plates 50, 36, 16, 46.

6. In the original edition of *Small Endearments* (Fox, 1985, 60–61), I discuss the comparison between the popularity of these swag borders and that image on eighteenth-century wallpapers, imported at great expense from France and England, and the less expensive alternative, that of an itinerant craftsman's stenciled motif on plain white walls. In *Wrapped in Glory* I point also to the preference of the Federal period for all-white surfaces transferred to the elegantly quilted swag and ribbon border on an 1805 Philadelphia quilt. During the second quarter of the nineteenth century, a trompe l'oeil valance was roller-printed on cotton in an arrangement of Roman draperies and swags (illustrated in Schoeser, *English and American Textiles,* p. 95). The simplified swag and tassel arrangement on this quilt, coupled with the number of similar portraits on which the suggestion of drapery appears, seems to suggest an additional stylistic source.

65. Fourth quarter nineteenth century
37³/₄ x 36 in. (95.9 x 91.4 cm)
Collection of The Newark Museum, gift of Mrs.
Ralph M. Wiggin, 1977

*B*OTANICAL

IMAGES

*O*f his father's Michigan farm in 1837, William Nowlin remembered that when their heavily timbered land had been cleared, a great oak tree had "escaped the fatal ax":

On account of its greatness, and its having so nice a body, father let it stand as monarch of the clearing. . . . [Its] roots were immense. They had been centuries creeping and feeling their way along, extracting life from mother earth to sustain their gigantic body. The acorn, from which that oak grew, must have been planted long before, and the tree which grew from it have been dressed many times in its summer robe of green, and it was, doubtless, flourishing when the "Mayflower" left the English Channel.[1]

Flourishing indeed! From Pennsylvania, in 1684, Francis Daniel Pastorius had written with astonishment to his parents in Germany, "I heartily wish for a dozen sturdy Tyrolese to fell the mighty oaks, for whichever way one turns it is *Itur in antiquam sylvam,* everything is forest."[2]

As with William Nowlin, children's memories of those giant trees were recalled almost reverentially. Whether uncut or shaped into the uneven floorboards beneath his feet, worked in strips to form his mother's apple basket, or incorporated into the great Conestoga wagons, the oak tree was part of the lives of child, quiltmaker, and community.

Almost from the country's beginnings the oak was synonymous with strength and with the continuity of life. If a quiltmaker had consciously sought symbolic imagery, she could hardly have chosen a motif more appropriate or meaningful for a child's quilt. Similarly inspired by the piney woods, when quiltmakers began to stitch small geometric

66. Saddlebrook, New Jersey
Mid-nineteenth century
40 x 40 in. (101.6 x 101.6 cm)
Collection of Jeannette Fink

In its earliest arrangement, four oak leaves (cut symmetrically from folded cotton) extend from a common center; in a more ambitious variation, this motif joins with the elements of another early pattern, the Reel. Two Oak Leaf and Reel patterns worked onto children's quilts attest to the inventiveness of nineteenth-century quiltmakers in their application of individual expression to the same traditional pattern. In the first (See illustration 65), the strength and physical texture of the oak tree have been ingeniously simulated through the choice of fabric, a sturdy, deep brown printed cotton, worked in appliqué and reverse appliqué and very tightly quilted.[3] On the other (See illustration 66), worked mid-century in Saddlebrook, New Jersey, a quiltmaker surrounded a similar, but more daintily executed, Oak Leaf and Reel with a Trailing Vine border. Then, as if to confirm her mastery of all the quiltmaking techniques, she completed her work with a wide border of Carolina Lily, pieced and appliquéd and one of the most-often-worked geometric floral patterns.

On children's quilts, oak leaves also appeared in tiny quilted stitches or as appliquéd motifs in multiple borders. They were also worked as single motifs (See illustration 67), suggesting, as does a blue and white Pennsylvania piece (See illustration 68), the pages of those botanical notebooks that held pressed or penciled records of American forests and fields.[4]

Botanical observations were imperative for the early arrivals in the colonies. The plants they found or fostered were used for food, medicine, shelter, and clothing; and the survival and the success of both settlers and settlements depended on the identification and utilization of the country's natural resources. However, by the nineteenth

shapes of fabric into an American tradition of pieced quilts, they arranged light and dark triangles into a stylized Pine Tree pattern. With only occasional exceptions, however, its small, sharp shapes seem to have been reserved for the pleasure of parents, and the pattern is seldom found on nineteenth-century quilts for children. Indeed, the Oak Leaf itself seems to appear on those small surfaces in only slightly larger numbers, although it appears with considerable consistency on larger quilts where it would seem to have been one of the oldest of the appliquéd patterns.

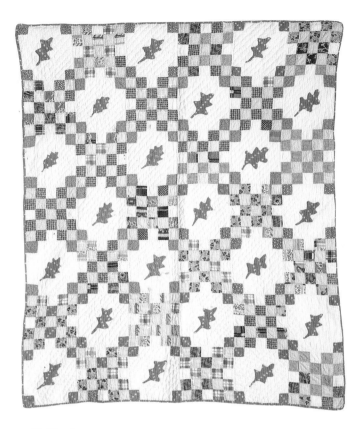

67. Third quarter nineteenth century
39 x 34 in. (99.1 x 86.4 cm)
Collection of Linda Reuther/Hearts and Hands/San Anselmo, California

68. Pennsylvania
Third quarter nineteenth century
35¼ x 34 in. (89.5 x 86.4 cm)
Collection of Stella Rubin Antiques, Potomac, Maryland

century, botany had become fashionable as well as functional. In that tradition, and in the images she cut from chintz to appliqué onto pagelike blocks, Mary Price's mother had collected a variety of floral specimens for another type of botanical notebook. We do not know if Mary was small or grown when this quilt was worked and given, for we know that women did present to their married daughters quilts intended to cover the mothers' own anticipated infants (See illustration 51, "A Common Vocabulary"). Nevertheless, with that quilt (See illustration 69), the child for whom those flowers

were gathered would be surrounded by the pastoral images that so frequently surrounded young children in the portraits and illustrations rendered by more formal artists of the period. The images in the watercolor landscape (See illustration 70), in which two small girls were painted, were those motifs chosen by a New Jersey quiltmaker four decades later: birds, butterflies, and blossoms, all for little "Flora" (See illustration 71), to whom the work is inscribed.

A rationale for the introduction of botany into a girl's school curriculum was set forth in 1829:

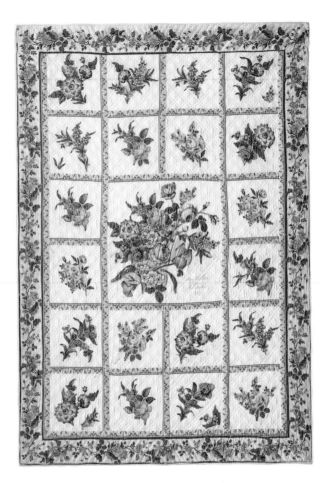

69. Inscribed, "Mary E. Price, from her Mother"
Pennsylvania
1847 (dated)
48 x 33 in. (121.9 x 83.8 cm)
Collection of Cynthia V. A. and Robert T.
Schaffner

Botany . . . is admirably adapted to the tastes, feelings, and capacities of females, as is demonstrated by the fact that the majority of botanists are females. Boys are less easily interested in it; more apt to be careless and harsh in their treatment of specimens, and too much attached to rude and boisterous sports. Girls, on the contrary, are apt to take delight in examining the most minute peculiarities of flowers, in pressing and preserving specimens and in delineating the most remarkable with the lead pencil, or in water colours. Their enthusiasm, therefore, will generally be easily awakened.[5]

That enthusiasm was also awakened and pursued in areas less academic and refined. Letters and diaries of young girls, particularly those on the frontier, were filled with countings and comparisons. For young Luna Warner, newly arrived in Kansas in 1871, the opportunities for informal botanical pursuits seem to have been endless. From her diary, we know that Luna enjoyed drawing from an eclectic assortment of published illustrations: "She brought me a pair of calfskin shoes and Viola's book *Eminent Women,* for me to draw out of" (June 24, 1872); "I finished the picture,

70. Joseph H. Davis
    Circa 1835
    Watercolor and pencil on paper
    7¾ x 10⅛ in. (19.5 x 26 cm)
    Copyright © Sotheby's, Inc.

'Sounds of the Alps,' and commenced another little picture" (January 19, 1872).[6]

For whatever reasons, her botanical interests seemed to be more in the recording
than in the rendering. After snow-filled
nights in borrowed dugouts and small cab-
ins, on March 18, 1871, the men in her parents' party began to establish claims and
Luna recorded, "There are 3 kinds of flowers in bloom here. We bathed for the first
time since we started from home [Massa-
chusetts]." On April 10 she wrote, "I have
found 8 kinds of flowers here. The cabin is
full of mice."[7]

The count continues: "I found some
flowers like verbenas. It makes 20 kinds
that I have found" (May 5); "I found a dan-
delion. We have found 37 kinds of flowers"
(May 20); by June 8, Luna had turned sixteen, they had slept in their new house, she
had found 71 kinds of flowers (including
"a sensitive plant in blossom" on June 2),
and she and her papa were planting corn
and teaching a calf to drink; on July 22,
Luna and her cousin Velma walked across
the prairie to climb to the top of Oak Creek
bluff, where they "had a cucumber that we
dug out for a water cup" and where she

71. Appliquéd inscription, "Flora"
    New Jersey
    1874 (dated)
    50 x 48 in. (127 x 121.9 cm)
    Private collection
    Photograph courtesy of America Hurrah Antiques,
    NYC

72. Second quarter nineteenth century
31½ x 31 in. (80 x 78.7 cm)
Private collection
Photograph courtesy of America Hurrah
Antiques, NYC

73. Third quarter nineteenth century
45 x 42 in. (114.3 x 106.7 cm)
Private collection
Photograph courtesy of America Hurrah
Antiques, NYC

found the two new kinds of flowers that brought her total to 117![8] By July 7, 1872, "The sunflowers around the old cabin are more than seven feet high. I measured one that was seven inches around."[9] Although huge sunflowers had been worked on earlier eastern quilts (See illustration 72), inspired by the all-white surfaces of America's Federal period, surely Luna would have been delighted to find that bright new varieties of sunflowers (See illustration 73) had adapted to the changing climate of American quilts.[10]

Rural or refined, botanical images bloomed across the entire spectrum of America's smallest quilts. The clusters of grapes and currants hanging with twisting leaves and curling tendrils from the sinuous interwoven branches of an elegant stenciled velvet theorem (See illustration 74), circa 1825, are the same motifs repeated on quilt blocks and borders throughout the nineteenth century. They were worked according to the whim of the quiltmaker in modest or magnificent numbers. Soutache (a very narrow braid popular on children's clothes of the period) is used on two of these (See illustrations 75 and 76), as the running vine sparsely surrounding the hexagons on the first, and as the stems on the lush fruits and berries sheltered in the undulating vines on the second. It was the pleasure of a Mechanicsburg, Pennsylvania, quiltmaker to construct her Cherry Wreath quilt (See illustration 77) on a perhaps recently acquired sewing machine; and small clusters of that same fruit were tucked into the multiple motifs applied by hand to the surface of a quilt presented to J. Miller Merritt February 8, 1860 (See illustration 78).

Pieced petals formed the Carolina Lily and the Peony, but it was the appliquéd rose and the tulip that appeared most often in classic patterns or in individual interpre-

74. "Grapevine"
Circa 1825
Paint on velvet
$14^7/_8$ x $22^7/_8$ (37.8 x 58.1 cm)
Abby Aldrich Rockefeller Folk Art Center

75. Third quarter nineteenth century
33 x 32 in. (83.8 x 81.3 cm)
Ex collection Phyllis Haders

76. Second quarter nineteenth century
    62½ x 42 in. (158 x 106.7 cm)
    The Brooklyn Museum 59.151.8, gift of Mrs. Alice
    Bauer Frankenberg

77. Mechanicsburg, Pennsylvania
    Third quarter nineteenth century
    27 x 25 in. (68.6 x 63.5 cm)
    Los Angeles County Museum of Art, gift of Felicia
    Melero Holtzinger

78. Inscribed in ink, "Presented to J. Miller Merritt
February 8, 1860"
Probably Pennsylvania
1860 (dated)
30 x 35 in. (76 x 89 cm)
Collection of Herb Wallerstein

tation. Although the rose had been a favored source of imagery for centuries of artists and authors (Shakespeare referred to it more than sixty times), early botanists seem not to have shared that creative enthusiasm. Only fourteen types of roses appeared in La Quintinie's 1690 *Herball,* in contrast to the listing of more than four hundred varieties of tulips; sixty years later Linnaeus wrote of only twenty varieties.

All this changed in the nineteenth century with the introduction of a number of new roses, especially the first hybrid tea varieties. Now an interest pursued fervently,

roses appeared as the single plantings in fashionable gardens; as embellishment on nineteenth-century costume; and appliquéd, padded, and embroidered, spilling out from the elegant urns and epergnes of Baltimore's Album quilts. But it was the simplest suggestion of those multipetaled motifs that became a standard decorative device on America's appliquéd quilts. The Foundation Rose was usually cut from triple-folded cloth into an eight-scallop circle, used singly (See illustration 79), or layered with increasingly smaller, multicolored, repetitive units, incorporated into

79. Third quarter nineteenth
century
38 x 32 in. (96.5 x 81.3 cm)
Private collection
*Photograph courtesy of America
Hurrah Antiques, NYC*

80. Franklin County, Ohio
Third quarter nineteenth century
41³/₄ x 39¹/₄ in. (106.1 x 99.7 cm)
Private collection

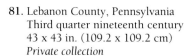

81. Lebanon County, Pennsylvania
Third quarter nineteenth century
43 x 43 in. (109.2 x 109.2 cm)
Private collection

82. Third quarter nineteenth century
46 x 39 in. (116.8 x 99.1 cm)
Private collection
Photograph courtesy of America
Hurrah Antiques, NYC

83. Gettysburg, Pennsylvania
Third quarter nineteenth century
38³/₄ x 35¹/₂ in. (98.4 x 90.2 cm)
Private collection
Courtesy of Stella Rubin

almost endlessly inventive surface designs (See illustrations 80, 81, and 82).

There was an occasional effort to miniaturize the complete surface area of a full-size quilt, as with this sampler (See illustration 83) on which the quiltmaker has appliquéd a border in which long vines flow out from a low basket, not unlike that which might be worked on a full-size quilt of similar, though larger, blocks.[11] But the reduced surfaces of the smaller quilts encouraged aesthetic experimentations that continue to suggest to the contemporary viewer the sense of whimsy and joy with

which they were surely sewn (See illustrations 84, 85, and 86).

Even the most individual efforts, however, were developed from wider aesthetic and social influences, and this is particularly true in the bold, bright, botanical images of Pennsylvania quilts. For nineteenth-century quiltmakers beyond Philadelphia, the influence of European folk traditions is more evident than the influence of European textiles. The seventeenth-century German settlers who came to participate in William Penn's great experiment brought with them not only the bitter

84. Pennsylvania
Fourth quarter nineteenth century
43¼ x 42¼ in. (109.9 x 107.3 cm)
Private collection

85. Third quarter nineteenth century
    38 x 33½ in. (96.5 x 85.1 cm)
    Private collection
    Photograph courtesy of America Hurrah Antiques,
    NYC

86. Attributed to Alma Richter
    Possibly Sunman, Ripley County, Indiana
    Possibly 1854
    45⅛ x 35⅛ in. (114.6 x 89.2 cm)
    Abby Aldrich Rockefeller Folk Art Center

memory of persecution, but also a sweeter ethnic memory of color and design. This was reflected in their regional folk art and, eventually, in their quilts.

The traditions and techniques craftsmen carried across the Atlantic were reworked into the American scene, although usually simplified to meet the demands of a new physical environment. One such craftsman was Daniel Pabst, a German cabinetmaker who acknowledged the source of his creative wellspring: "I brought all of Germany with me, in my inward eye."[12] The motifs that were stored in those collective inward

eyes were translated to paper and wood, to metal and clay, and much later to cotton quilts.

A Pennsylvania child's first exposure to the colors and shapes of that visual heritage might well have been in *Frakturschriften* or *Fraktur*-writing. This decorative calligraphy was embellished in a distinctive palette of flat washes carried by cat's hair brushes onto the carefully inked outlines of designs still associated with the region, such as tulips and parrots. It was one of the dominant forces in the development of the visual folk traditions of that state. Its techniques were based in the illuminated manuscripts of European religious communities where printing techniques and woodblocks had now increasingly displaced the need for penmanship and handdrawn illustration.

We see the tradition reemerge in Pennsylvania, primarily in secular form. A piece of *Fraktur* may have been the work of a local schoolmaster or of an itinerant craftsman now identifiable only through his individual preferences for motifs or by the geographic regions of his activities: the Flying Angel Artist, the Mount Pleasant Artist,

the Sussex-Washington Artist. The limner would paint the image of the infant; the *Fraktur*-writer would record the events of his life in the *Taufscheine,* which recorded his birth and baptism, and in the *Vorschriften,* which rewarded his youthful accomplishments and good behavior with illustrated moral directives (See illustration 87): "Children / obey your Parents in the Lord: for this is right. / Honour thy Father and Mother which is the first / commandment with promise, That it may be well with thee, and thou mayest live long on the earth." The importance of, and apprecia-

87. Vorschrift
From the Hostetter Collection, Franklin &
Marshall College, Lancaster, Pennsylvania

88. Centerport, Berks County, Pennsylvania
Fourth quarter nineteenth century
42 x 42 in. (106.7 x 106.7 cm)
*Collection of Rosemarie B. and Richard S.
Machmer*

tion for, even small and naive examples of these commendations is indicated by the large number that have survived, tucked away in the pages of Bibles or other books.

The tulip is perhaps the most visible symbol in Pennsylvania German folk design, and it flourished on Pennsylvania quilts (See illustration 88). After its introduction to Europe from Asia Minor in the middle of the sixteenth century, the tulip became the flower of fashion. *Tulipenwuth* ("tulip-madness") swept the continent as huge fortunes were made and lost with the buying and selling of bulbs. In the eighteenth century, the use of the tulip as a decorative motif on the slip- and sgraffito-decorated earthenware was pervasive throughout the pottery of Germany's Palatinate Valley. Surely it was a design and skill brought to Pennsylvania by the potters from that region, who were probably among the waves of immigrants. We know that in Europe the tulip was viewed as a variation of the Holy Lily, its three petals symbolizing the Trinity. However, like the great circular configurations on the barns of Berks and Lehigh counties, what meaning it may have had for those early craftsmen and artists is unclear. On quilts, there is little to suggest it was applied for any other reason than the quiltmaker's delight in its decorative possibilities.

In the history of American quilts, those of distinctly Pennsylvania German design came rather late. Prior to 1850, the Pennsylvania *hausfrau's* featherbeds generally displayed the product of the weaver's loom rather than of the quilter's frame. The woven coverlet was a symbol of pride in the tradition of excellence that had been established by the first group of weavers who arrived in Germantown; but the pattern

89. Inscribed in ink, "Edna E. Meyer"
Pennsylvania
1881 (dated)
48¼ x 48¼ in. (122.6 x 122.6 cm)
Collection of Dr. and Mrs. Donald M. Herr

90. Eastern Pennsylvania
    Fourth quarter nineteenth century
    43 x 43 in. (109.2 x 109.2 cm)
    Collection of Rosemarie B. and Richard S.
    Machmer

books that were passed from father to son were eventually joined by the template patterns that were passed from mother to daughter.

The fold-and-cut technique that produced the Foundation Rose was a simplified version of *scherenschnitte*, an important technical element in the Pennsylvania folk tradition. In addition to the type of smaller scattered motifs cut for the surface of J. Miller Merritt's quilt (See illustration 78), it produced the large, stylized botanical images that appear on a Sawtooth Diamond with flowers and stars (See illustration 89) signed and dated (1881) by Edna E. Meyer in Lebanon County, and the large Cockscomb that often appeared in each of the four quadrants of full-size quilts. The Cockscomb pattern appeared in variation in almost every Pennsylvania county in which it was worked, but all shared certain design elements, including distinctive reverse-appliqué work on flowers and leaves. The border treatments on the leaves of this example (See illustration 90) relate to the use of *scherenschnitte* on the dropped borders of the paper shelf-linings of the area and the full pattern is almost identical to that on a full-size quilt worked in Cumberland County.[13] At least two other quiltmakers (in Northumberland and Snyder counties) worked the Cockscomb on children's quilts, each on a white ground and surrounded by an inner Sawtooth border.[14] The Pennsylvania quiltmakers' palettes and patterns were drawn from a common source, but on these smallest of quilts (See illustration 91) they often seem uniquely their own.

As traditions and techniques moved west, the quiltmaker took the Carolina Lily and the Foundation Rose with her, either

91. Third quarter nineteenth century
42 x 42 in. (106.7 x 106.7 cm)
Private collection
Photograph courtesy of America Hurrah Antiques, NYC

carefully folded and packed in her wagon, or (like Daniel Pabst) in her "inward eye." The young girls who had sketched the flowers in more familiar fields were now the women who moved into successively new frontiers.

> We have found the wild tulip, the primrose, the lupine, the ear-drop, the larkspur, and creeping holyhock, and a beautiful flower resembling the bloom of the beach tree, but in bunches as big as a small sugar-leaf, and of every variety of shade to red and green. I botanize and read some, but cook a "heap" more.[15]

These botanical observations were recorded on the way to California, in an 1846 letter written near the Platte River, 200 miles from Fort Laramie, by Tamsen Donner, for whom there would be no more gardens; she perished in the snow-covered Sierras.

Abigail Malick's journey brought her safely to the Oregon Territory, where her letters to the family and friends who remained behind characteristically asked for letters in return, and for photographs and seeds:

musk-mellone, greap, cabage, parcely, and flour seades . . . som good redish An Lettus and shougar peas . . . and bunch peas and enney sort of seades you have. . . . I am Agoing to Get som seades sent from pennsylvania [1853].[16]

The young sapling and the small garden in which this Nebraska family stands (See illustration 92) were the civilizing symbols of America's frontiers, where there were new quilts to be made, new seeds to be sewn.[17]

92. Photograph
Near Woods Park below Sargent, Nebraska, Custer County, 1886
Solomon D. Butcher Collection
Nebraska State Historical Society

NOTES

1. Nowlin, 181.

2. Garvan, 37. Pastorius was the Pennsylvania agent for the Frankfort Land Company and his arrival coincided with the first major German migration into America.

3. See illustration in Hoffman, 9, of a second child's quilt taken from the same unidentified pattern source that inspired this quilt. Cut from a Portuguese Pink printed cotton, its size and design vary only slightly from its New Jersey cousin.

4. Collections of pressed leaves appear in cotton on several full-size botanical quilts, including a bedcover (illustrated in Binney, 50) containing thirty-six individual New England specimens.

5. "Botany for Schools," *American Journal of Education,* 1829. The article may have been written by William Russell, who edited the journal from 1826 to 1829.

6. Warner, 417, 304.

7. Ibid., 280–281.

8. Ibid., 283–285, 288.

9. Ibid., 421.

10. Fox, *Wrapped in Glory,* 32–37. Similar whitework sunflowers appear on the top corners of an extremely sophisticated quilt worked by, for, or with Rachel DePuy in Philadelphia in 1805.

11. See Lasansky, *Heart of Pennsylvania,* 35, for illustration of an elaborated example of this type of border treatment on a full-size quilt.

12. Hanks and Talbott, 7.

13. See Lasansky, *Pieced by Mother,* 51, for illustration.

14. See Lasansky, *Heart of Pennsylvania,* 44, for illustration.

15. Holmes, 72.

16. Schlissel, Gibbens, and Hampsten, 29.

$\mathscr{T}$HE

HEAVENS

$\mathscr{S}$tars great and small shone brightly across this entire century of American quilts, and their multiple variations were translated intact from the beds of parents to the beds of children and dolls. As did the quilts themselves (See illustration 93), the stories of astronomical objects and events continued to pass from one generation to another: folklore and legend in the oral tradition of dimly remembered tales; allegory and symbolism found in more formal literature. Those objects and events that inspired illustration on cotton quilts were elegantly entered on a multitude of other decorative surfaces, such as the John Fisher case clock described in *The Maryland Gazette* (Baltimore) of September 10, 1790:

> [The clock] displays seconds, hours, months, and days, as well as the signs of the zodiac and the seven planets of the pre-Copernican system; its astronomical dial has a moon face and stars and a planispheric map of the northern hemisphere with sunrises and sunsets illustrated.[1]

In addition, they appeared in simpler form on the informative pages of the *Old Farmer's Almanac,* found hung on a nail or placed on a handy shelf in almost every home in the nation.

Laura Russell, born in 1827 in Plymouth, Massachusetts, recalled that the *Old Farmer's Almanac* and the Bible constituted the entire library of Mrs. Martha ("Marm") Weston, an elderly woman usually dressed in "an indigo blue calico gown with small white spots" in whose "dame school" she had been enrolled at a very early age. Laura's memories tell us that on top of the almanac

> was a small wooden box into which at the close of each day we dropped our little

93. Inscribed in ink, "When Ever the [illegible] Dearest [illegible] Think of Me. From Mary to Eliza."
Second quarter nineteenth century
46 x 46 in. (116.8 x 116.8 cm)
Collection of Jeannette Fink

94. Third quarter nineteenth century
21$^1/_2$ x 17$^1/_2$ in. (54.6 x 44.5 cm)
Collection of Muriel and David Greenberg
Courtesy of Nancy Glazer

brass thimbles and our bit of patchwork with its irregular, blackened stitches piled one upon another after having been many times picked out and re-sewed with squeaking, crooked needle and tear-dimmed eyes.[2]

The sky was a continuing source of wonder for intellectual and illiterate alike, and within their homes and immediate neighborhoods children would generally have been aware of a great diversity of astronomical theories and interpretations (See illustration 94). In addition to Marm's almanac, little Laura Russell's sources included an old sea captain who:

had a scientific turn of mind, and who among other pursuits, gave a great deal of time to astronomy. His ideas were somewhat peculiar; he believed our planet to be the center of the universe, and that the sun and moon and stars all revolved around it . . . my father many times argued the question with him, but never succeeded in convincing him that his theory was incorrect. The old man wrote a great many pages on this and other subjects and made numerous diagrams showing how the heavenly bodies were related to each other according to his ideas. At different times he lent my father these manuscripts to read, and we were much amused with the rude drawings and the extraordinary spelling which we found in them. One of them in particular contained a page covered with illustrations of the planetary system, the earth occupying a large space in the center, the orb of day being conspicuous for its absence. A small corner of the leaf was missing, and the old man had written in his crabbed characters around the ragged edge of the paper: "The sun's got tore out."[3]

Laura also recalled

a woman of strong common sense but ignorant, a believer in omens and somewhat given to prophesy. She used to look up the wide chimney of her dwelling and count the stars, predicting as many snowstorms for the winter as they numbered; but I am not aware that there was any particular time of the year or of the night that was devoted to these scientific observations.[4]

Another Massachusetts child, Lucy Larcom, observed that "regularly everyday" an elderly shoemaker from the small shop that adjoined her father's would come out and "stand for a long time at the corner, motionless as a post, with his nose and chin pointing skyward, usually to the northeast. I watched his face with wonder, for it was said that 'Uncle John' was 'weatherwise,' and knew all the secrets of the heavens."[5]

These tales and images, and the sky itself, were familiar objects to nineteenth-century children. Had they wished to find comparative images, they would perhaps need look no further than the surfaces of the quilts that covered them or upon which they dozed. ("If a baby's head nodded, a little bed was made for it on a soft 'comforter' in the corner where it had its nap out undisturbed.")[6] Even on the smallest of doll quilts (See illustration 95), needle and thread recorded a set of principal patterns

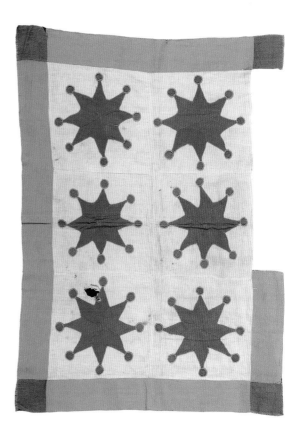

95. Third quarter nineteenth century
23 x 16⅞ in. (58.4 x 42.9 cm)
Private collection

through which women and their daughters (See illustration 96) illustrated the firmament. Their interpretations were primarily intuitive rather than intellectual, although astronomy clubs attained a certain popularity both for children and adults. Young Luna Warner identified "2 sun dogs, very bright and a rainbow-colored circle around the sun and just the same around the moon all evening."[7] Even in the late 1800s *The Girl's Home Companion* lamented:

The charm of a still, clear starlight night is felt, we believe, by every one possessed of the least culture or taste; but the number at present is very few of those young girls who can call the brilliant orbs by their names, and look intelligently on the starry heavens. And yet no science is more sublime or captivating than Astronomy; it appeals to our highest faculties; to our fancy and imagination.[8]

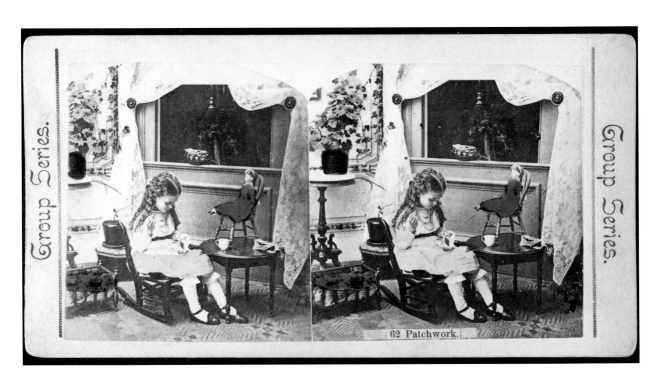

96. Undated stereograph
"Patchwork"
Private collection

Among the most basic of those patterns were the same linear arrangements drawn by every culture in which an artisan sought to work creatively within a square. Worked on American quilts they became known, at some point, as Variable Star, Evening Star, and LeMoyne Star (See illustration 97), but even those classic names often yielded, if only temporarily, to regional or commercial designations.[9] By whatever name those patterns eventually came to be known, each shares the true astronomical characteristics of stars known as variable stars that "vary in brightness, and frequently in other respects as well. These variations are fluctuations so that they do not permanently alter the configurations of the stars.[10] *The Girl's Home Companion* had brought this to the attention of its young readers in its chapter on "Starlight Nights": "There are also variable stars which change in size at different times."[11]

The quiltmakers' choices of color and dimension and placement have at particular moments made each block ordinary or extravagant, brilliant or drab. As each approached the same configuration she sought, nevertheless, to find another "fluctuation" through her own hands, occasionally simulating the twinkling effect of those stars through variations in the pattern's outer line, variations that eventually came to be called a Feathered Star (See illustrations 98 and 99) or Sawtooth Star (See illustration 100). In addition to the tidy containment of individual stars within individual blocks (a method of design and construction that came to characterize the American pieced quilt) (See illustrations 101 and 102), the size and splendor of the heavens were suggested more specifically in massive star motifs that radiated as single units from the center of full-size quilts. Each star was composed of eight

97. Second quarter nineteenth century
36½ x 33 in. (92.7 x 83.8 cm)
Los Angeles County Museum of Art, gift of Felicia Melero Holtzinger

98. Fourth quarter nineteenth century
36 x 36 in. (91.4 x 91.4 cm)
Private collection
Photograph courtesy of America Hurrah Antiques,
NYC

99. Probably Vermont
   Third quarter nineteenth century
   44 x 44¼ in. (111.8 x 112.4 cm)
   Private collection

100. Second quarter nineteenth century
    42 x 40 in. (106.7 x 101.6 cm)
    *Collection of Stella Rubin Antiques, Potomac,
    Maryland*

large diamonds, with each of those diamonds composed of hundreds of smaller diamonds in a significant number of early chintz and printed cottons. Particularly in the first decades of the century, these stars were worked in magnificent dimension across quilts often nine feet square or larger. To an admiring quiltmaker of perhaps less talent and persistence, the sight of such a star spread across a bed would surely result in feelings of no less awe and reverence than she might have felt if she were looking upward into clear, dark skies. "Was it not indispensable to her peace of mind that her 'blazing star of Mexico' should blaze more brilliantly than that of her neighbor?"[12]

The perfect construction of those immense motifs required a high degree of technical excellence. ("Would someone kindly tell through these [periodical] columns how to piece an old fashioned blazing star quilt, such as our grandmothers used to piece years ago, and oblige a farmer's wife?")[13] That they were reduced in scale and worked for a child's small bed (See illustrations 103 and 104) attests to the fact that no pattern was considered too difficult to work into those small endearments.

A sense of confidence in the dependability of the heavens was of particular importance to the daily life of a primarily agrarian society (See illustration 105). A comfortable continuity in the timeliness of

101. Second quarter nineteenth century
39³/₄ x 34¹/₂ in. (101 x 87.6 cm)
The Fine Arts Museums of San Francisco,
Museum purchase, funds from Foundation
owned objects sold at auction, 1990.9.1.

things is confirmed in the recording of nineteenth-century childhood and in the frequent association of the cycles of childhood with the changing of the seasons. Evelyn Ward recalled her childhood at Bladensfield, Virginia:

> We children had our jobs, any number of them. There was the sage to be picked for the sausage, the golden crab apples to be gathered for jelly, bags of chinquapins to be gotten in the warm sunshine behind the barn.
>
> After frost came, chestnuts would be dropping freely. We would have to be out early every morning to pick them up before the hogs could get around to the trees and gather them for us. Often while out picking up nuts we would see the great red sun rising in the Autumn mist.
>
> Our biggest job was to pick the cotton, but that would wait till November when the cotton balls would open. Father always raised a small supply of cotton that was picked by the children of the place, black and white. . . . Every summer we spent hours and hours paring fruit— peaches, quinces and apples—to be dried for winter use; now it was put in bags and spread along the windows on a sloping roof to catch the sun.[14]

102. Second quarter nineteenth century
39 x 39 in. (99.1 x 99.1 cm)
Shelburne Museum, Shelburne, Vermont

Sometimes the seasons went awry (a frost too early, a drought too long), as did the seasons of young lives. As the younger children of Bladensfield were building warm memories of happy days in green orchards, the country was poised on the edge of a great civil war. Before the seasons had once again gone full circle, Evelyn's Brother Will would be dead and Brother Charlie, not yet eighteen, would be shot in their beloved Virginia fields.

From the "dim half-memory" of her infancy, Lucy Larcom remembered:

103. Inscribed with gold-colored floss,
"M. A. Michel"
Western Pennsylvania
Fourth quarter nineteenth century
46 x 45 in. (116.8 x 114.3 cm)
Private collection

the surprise [the stars] were to me, seen for the first time. One evening, just before I was put to bed, I was taken in somebody's arms—my sister's, I think—outside the door, and lifted up under the dark, still, clear sky, splendid with stars, thicker and nearer earth than they have ever seemed since. All my little being shaped itself into a subdued, delighted "Oh!" And then the exultant thought flitted through the mind of the reluctant child, as she was carried in, "Why, *that* is the roof of the house I live in."[15]

If the sky could seem comfortably familiar, it could also burst forth with frightening inconsistencies. Not surprisingly, and particularly in the experiences of children on the western frontier, storms were remembered in terrible detail. During his boyhood journey to Oregon in 1843, Jesse Applegate recalled:

I suddenly awoke. The rain was pouring down into my face, my eyes were blinded with the glare of lightning, the wind was

104. Fourth quarter nineteenth century
35$\frac{1}{2}$ x 33$\frac{1}{2}$ in. (90.2 x 85.1 cm)
Collection of Herb Wallerstein

105. Mid-nineteenth century
40 x 40 in. (101.6 x 101.6 cm)
Collection of Gail Binney-Stiles

roaring like a furnace, and the crash of thunder was terrible and almost continuous. I could see nothing but what looked like sheets of fire, and hear nothing but the wind, the pouring rain, and the bellowing thunder.[16]

Storms, while fearful, were nevertheless a familiar phenomenon. There were other, more ominous occasions, unfamiliar and inexplicable; and authors, astronomers, and artists had always recorded those moments. In A.D. 1054, Chinese and Japanese astronomers recorded a supernova (a massive explosion of a star) that seems also to have been recorded by Native Americans on a Mimbres burial pot.[17] The 1066 appearance of Halley's Comet was stitched onto the Bayeux Tapestry in a vignette captioned "They are in awe of the star." The comet's arrival in 1301 had inspired Giotto

106. Probably New England
Third quarter nineteenth century
48 x 48 in. (121.9 x 121.9 cm)
Ex Binney collection

to paint its presence in his depiction of the Adoration of the Magi in a series of frescoes in the Scrovegni Chapel in Padua. "The Early Comets," published in an 1898 edition of the *Essex Antiquarian* records several contemporary responses to comets seen over New England in the second half of the seventeenth century:

> "The great and dreadful comet," as Josselyn called it, was first seen on the eighth of November [1664]. Night after night, the whole winter through, "the great blazing starre" took its position in the southern sky as soon as the stars began to glint in the evening constellations.
>
> Increase Mather gave a lecture [on the Newtonian comet of 1680], saying in his introduction that "As for this blazing star, which hath occasioned this discourse, it was a terrible sight indeed."
>
> The governor and council of the Massachusetts Bay colony appointed a general fast, one reason for it in the proclamation being ". . . that awful, portentous, blazing star, usually foreboding some calamity to the beholder thereof."[18]

In the eighteenth century, Eliza Pinckney described to a girlhood friend the reappearance over South Carolina of Newton's comet:

> The comett had the appearance of a very large Starr with a tail, and to my sight about 5 or 6 foot long, its real magnitude must then be prodigious. . . . The brightness of the Comett was too dazzling for mee to give you the information you require.[19]

A remarkable group of comets presented themselves throughout the nineteenth century, and among the most spectacular meteor showers of modern times were those that occurred in 1833 and 1866. At the peak of the 1833 display, ten thousand meteors per hour were visible over the eastern United States. America's most powerful and enigmatic recordings of these and other major meteorological events appear with primarily biblical images on two late nineteenth-century full-size quilts worked in Georgia by Harriet Powers (1837–1911). Among the occurrences illustrated on her extraordinary figurative narratives are: "The falling of the stars on November 13, 1833. The people were frighten and thought that the end of time had come"; "The darkness over the earth and the moon turning into blood"; "The dark day of May 19, 1780. The seven stars were seen 12.N. in the day. . . . The sun went off to a small spot and then to darkness"; and "The stare that appeared in 1886 for the first time in three hundred years."[20]

The great "Blazing Starre" quilts that were visible on American beds throughout the nineteenth century were in all probability worked independently of any specific event or occurrence. Nevertheless the strength of the images invites remarkable comparisons to the single, spectacular moments of energy, and those Starbursts (See illustration 106) were worked in less fearful proportion onto smaller surfaces to cover American children in similar splendor.

NOTES

1. Garvan, 62.
2. Russell, 22.
3. Ibid., 31.
4. Ibid., 18.
5. Larcom, 40.
6. Ibid., 42.
7. Warner, 297.
8. Valentine, 577.

9. A number of periodicals and mail-order pattern companies were among those late nineteenth- and early twentieth-century sources contributing to an increasing emphasis on the naming of quilt patterns. See Brackman, 106–114.

10. Baker, 334.
11. Valentine, 579.
12. *Good Housekeeping,* 263.
13. Colcord, 18.
14. Ward, 13–14.
15. Larcom, 46–47.
16. Applegate, 14–15.
17. Dye, A3, A18.
18. *Essex Antiquarian,* 75.
19. Pinckney, *Diary,* 35.

20. See Fox, *Wrapped in Glory,* 136–141, for illustrations of and text about Harriet Powers's Bible quilt in the Smithsonian Institution and The Creation of the Animals quilt in the collection of the Museum of Fine Arts in Boston.

107. Kees Homestead, New York
Third quarter nineteenth century
59$\frac{1}{2}$ x 51$\frac{1}{2}$ in. (151.1 x 130.8 cm)
Collection of Dr. and Mrs. Roger L. Lerner

FLYING GEESE

Few of those natural occurrences linked to the skies and to the seasons were as consistent and as visual as the migrations of great flocks of wild geese.

The direction those journeys took through the skyways had been set long ago. Just as a child and his parents might follow ruts worn deep in the Oregon Trail leading to the Pacific Ocean, so too did those other migrations follow routes already explored, airy paths that were remembered to offer food, water, and finally, it was hoped, safe haven. The Ross's goose flew south across the plains, then turned west near Great Falls, Montana, to cross the Rocky Mountains; the blue goose traveled 1,700 miles from Canada's James Bay to coastal Louisiana; others left their nesting grounds near Hudson Bay to feed in North Carolina from October until the first full moon in March.

Young Luna Warner's migration with her family brought her from their home near Barre, Massachusetts, to a homestead on the Solomon River south of Downs, Kansas, where she recorded in extraordinary numbers her botanical observations and, in smaller seasonal numbers, the great flocks of wild geese as they appeared over her Kansas skies. (Birds and blossoms had more colorfully been recorded on a child's quilt made on the Kees Homestead in New York [See illustration 107].) In 1871, Luna's sixteenth year, she recorded in her diary:

March 19. There are wild geese flying over every day. We are right in a prairie dog town.
October 4. Ever so many wild geese flew over. We heard cranes in the evening.

October 12. Ever so many geese went over. . . . Some stopped in the river.[1]

108. Stereograph (detail)
"Patchwork"
1889 (dated)
Private collection

Continuing in 1872, she wrote:

March 11. Louie shot a wild goose out on the prairies.
April 1. There are geese flying over all the time.
October 10. When I got home Louie had shot a wild goose and there was another flying around. At last it lit on the river and Louie went down and shot it. Ma baked them and had Arabella come over to supper.[2]

A child on the frontier remembered that "hunting seemed to me the greatest sport in all creation. Compared with [it] everything else was as dust in the cyclone."[3] While fathers and sons hunted the wild geese, we know that mothers and daughters were stitching for the flocks a measure of immortality (See illustration 108),[4] but whether by conscious choice or coincidence is seldom ascertainable.

Rufus Porter (1791–1884) painted the

109. Third quarter nineteenth century
48 x 42 in. (121.9 x 106.7 cm)
Collection of Darwin D. Bearley Antiques,
Akron, Ohio

American landscape in a series of murals on New England walls. Flying geese are rendered in simple, dark strokes, in umber monochrome, for example, on the Massachusetts walls of the Van Heusen farm in North Reading (circa 1835–40) and in polychrome on a panel in 1838 in the Westwood home of Dr. Francis Howe.[5] During those same decades, the simple dark V's suggested on the frescoes were being worked consistently in repetitive triangles of bright calico and chintz (See illustration 109). We do not know if they—and those that followed—were deliberate renderings or simple representations of the pleasure of pattern. Luna Warner, a quiltmaker even in her girlhood, might have been able to tell us, but she did not.

During the years Luna recorded those flowers and flying geese, she had also made detailed entries containing the titles of books and periodicals she was reading, and

110. Maryland
1880 (dated)
$39^{3}/_{4}$ x $37^{1}/_{2}$ in. (101 x 95.3 cm)
Collection of Adrienne and Howard Moss
Courtesy of Stella Rubin

111. Ohio
Third quarter nineteenth century
35 x 35 in. (88.9 x 88.9 cm)
Collection of Darwin D. Bearley Antiques,
Akron, Ohio

those that were being read to her, including: Whittier's poetry, *Harper's Magazine, The History of the War, The Virginians,* and a great deal of Dickens (*Nicholas Nickleby, David Copperfield, Oliver Twist, The Old Curiosity Shop,* and *Barnaby Rudge*). On July 29, 1871, for example, Alf (a relative of Luna's mother) had "started for Solomon City after my piano," and that evening "Ma read aloud in *Martin Chuzzlewit.*" The next evening "there came up the hardest thunder I ever saw. It rained so that you couldn't see an inch, thunder and lightning enough to blind and deafen anybody." When the

piano finally arrived on August 4, "They unloaded the piano and got it into the house. We all worked about all day getting it set up. It was soaking wet and the varnish spoiled but the inside is all right but needs tuning badly. I played all evening." Luna played her piano most of the following day, taking time out to draw and to eat sweet melon, and "Ma read some." On August 6, she commented that the piano "does not sound well at all. Ma finished reading *Martin Chuzzlewit.*"[6]

Luna also recorded her quiltmaking activities during those same years, but with

112. Third quarter nineteenth century
36 x 30 in. (91.4 x 76.2 cm)
Private collection

an uncharacteristic and exasperating lack of detail. On July 9, 1871, she noted, "I have 22 squares of an album bed quilt done."[7] On January 3, 1872, she "commenced a delaine bed quilt."[8] On the following day, "I sewed patchwork in the evening."[9] Did the blocks of her album quilt contain appliquéd renderings of her floral discoveries? Did her "patchwork" include those rows of triangles that appeared with great frequency on America's pieced quilts? If it did, had Luna called them Fly-

ing Geese? Did she even consider, let alone acknowledge, that she had worked in tight abstraction those shapes she had recorded elsewhere with pen on paper?

While those shapes had become, through oral tradition or written word, the quiltmaker's favorite flock, the triangle had long been worked into multiple units that offered the opportunity for a great diversity of arrangement and pattern. Did rows turned inward suggest to her the wild geese that landed to compete for food in a great

113. New York
Second quarter nineteenth century
41 x 38 in. (104.1 x 96.5 cm)
The Baltimore Museum of Art, gift of Linda and
Irwin Berman, St. Simons Island, Georgia
Photograph courtesy of Thos. K. Woodard
American Antiques & Quilts

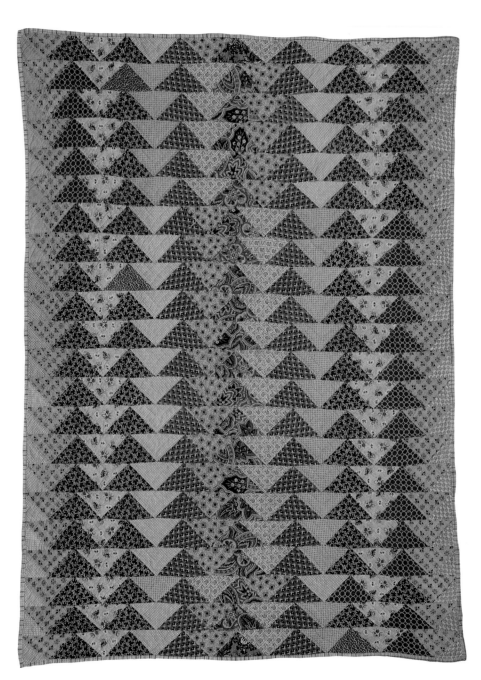

114. New England
Second quarter nineteenth century
38 x 27 in. (96.5 x 68.6 cm)
Collection of Frank and Lucy Flanigan

stubbled field, a Wild Goose Chase (See illustrations 110 and 111)? Flocks were seen not only in the sky but also in the fields where they fed or in the middle of cold dark ponds where they felt safe. (Luna's brother, Louis, had shot one on the prairie, and Luna had seen them in the river.) The special sounds and signals they gave forth as they fed were soon replaced with shrill honking, an announcement that the flock was about to resume flight. Or was it a quieter comparison? Did a quiltmaker see in them the domestic goose, descended from the greylags, about whom she sang to her drowsy children, "Go tell Aunt Rhody / Go tell Aunt Rhody / Her old gray goose is dead / The one she was saving / To make her feather bed"? (See illustration 112).

Whatever those shapes were called, and for whatever reason they were worked, nineteenth-century quilts for children and dolls provide a rich repository of individual interpretations and manipulations. For example, on one small quilt (See illustration 113), tiny lines of those great flocks seem to tug impatiently at a lingering star, as if they are anxious for the night to be gone and their long journey to begin again. Most often the simple triangles were repeated in row after row of Flying Geese (See illustration 114), long lines of the simple shapes Luna Warner had seen moving across that heartland sky.

NOTES

1. Warner, 280, 293, 294.
2. Warner, 307, 411, 428. Louie is Luna's brother and her only sibling; Arabella is her cousin.
3. West, 105.
4. "Mrs. Medley" is written across the bottom border of the 1889 stereograph from which this detail is taken; it is probably a reference to a character in popular literature. Among the decorative touches included in this scene are a crazy quilt cover on a small table and a ruffled, partially completed bit of pieced work, pinned to the back of a chair.
5. Lipman, plates 9 and 16.
6. Warner, 289. Alf refers to Alpheus Cleveland, distantly related to Luna's mother and one of the Warner party that traveled with them from Massachusetts.
7. Ibid., 287.
8. Warner, 301. See F. Montgomery, *Textiles in America*, 215–216. In an illustrated definition she identifies delaine as a fine woolen fabric that came into popularity in England about 1835 and was commonly found in log cabin quilts, "in which the wiry, hard cloth never lies quite flat and assumes a slightly tubular appearance."
9. Warner, 301.

$\mathscr{P}$IECED FOR PLEASURE

$\mathscr{W}$hereas elegant English chintz and the more privileged classes determined the stylistic characteristics of many of our earliest quilts and bedcovers, it was eventually simpler, store-bought cottons and women of the middle class that produced an extraordinary number of block-style pieced quilts that for many came to define the truly American quilt.

In the centuries preceding the Industrial Revolution there was an importance attached to textiles that is almost impossible for people of the twentieth century to assess or understand. In early America, any imported fabric was purchased at great expense and the cloth a woman used for her household linen and her family's apparel was most often the product of her own labor. The piece of fabric bought not with money but with work was something to view with special respect, every inch tangible proof of the extent of her efforts. Even after the Industrial Revolution had put comparatively less expensive printed cottons into the hands of an expanding market, the production of homespun continued apace, and it did so, for a variety of reasons, well into the last half of the nineteenth century.

The record of the participation of children in the multiple tasks associated with the production of cloth was certainly a record of childhood denied for many orphans and for many children of the poor, who carded and spun in workhouses in colonial America. But in the nineteenth century, a child's participation in home manufactures, if often hard and boring, was not so different from other work. Their efforts were considered an economic advantage, additionally reinforcing the concept of the family as a unit in which each must perform for the good of the whole.

115. Second quarter nineteenth century
44 x 40¾ in. (111.8 x 103.5 cm)
*The Metropolitan Museum of Art, Friends of
the American Wing Fund, 1989 (1989.255)*

116. Undated photograph
Written on reverse: "Helen Winebremmer/
and/ her cousin."
Private collection

The pride in self-sufficiency that Brigham Young had instilled in his followers was noted by Emma Carroll Seegmiller as she set down what she remembered of her youth in the United Order of Orderville, Utah. In addition to homespun garments, the shoes she wore in that community were handmade in their entirety. They were tanned in their own tannery with hide from their own cattle, and using tannery bark from their own trees. Thus "topped off with our homemade straw hats, we became vividly distinctive, as self made-up as even President Brigham Young might have wished."[2]

Not withstanding piety, patriotism, and practicality, home manufactures placed a visual limitation on what even the most creative could accomplish with clothing and quilts. Plain or plaid, striped or checked were the limited options available on the weaver's loom. Color was the only possible variation, and Emma remembered "those large dye pots of indigo blue and aniline. The wild greasewood when steeped made a good yellow dye; when mixed with the indigo blue it made a very pretty green."[3]

However, even Emma, a fervent young daughter of Zion, could not resist factory-made fabrics:

> The figured calicoes in varied colors and designs . . . seemed so sheer compared with our usual homespun. And the "shiny" buttons, the neatly folded papers of pins and cases of needles, the spools of thread, and best of all the "store smell" that went with it.[4]

In addition, homespun carried with it a variety of special political and social implications. During the Civil War, for example, Southern women considered homespun to be their own particular badge of honor, as it was for the Mormon settlers in Utah:

> For many years homespun woolen-linseys were all there was to wear. Brigham Young at one time decreed that men mustn't dance with any one in other than homespun garments; this was to discourage vanities and extravagances and to encourage home manufactures.[1]

117. Fourth quarter nineteenth century
$36^{1}/_{2}$ x $36^{1}/_{2}$ in. (92.7 x 92.7 cm)
Collection of Muriel and David Greenberg

118. Pennsylvania
Fourth quarter nineteenth century
45 x 45 in. (114.3 x 114.3 cm), reverse, detail
Private collection

Particularly during the last half of the nineteenth century, it was those "figured calicoes," many colored with the newly invented aniline dyes and increasingly of American manufacture, that were worked into inventive surface compositions of blocks and borders. The pieced patterns selected for a child's quilt were usually no different from those the quiltmaker might have selected for her own. The curved-seam pattern on a Pennsylvania child's quilt (See illustration 115) is identical, save for scale, to that included in the setting in which Baby Helen and her cousin have been photographed (See illustration 116). Propped beneath a tree in that quilt-covered chair, both children and quilt have been carefully arranged for the photo-

119. A note attached to this quilt reads,
"This is Grandpa R's cradle quilt. Aunt Lilla"
Maine
Fourth quarter nineteenth century
41$\frac{1}{2}$ x 39 in. (105.4 x 99.1 cm)
Pilgrim/Roy Collection

120. Possibly Block Island, Rhode Island
Fourth quarter nineteenth century
37¼ x 31¼ in. (94.6 x 79.4 cm)
Abby Aldrich Rockefeller Folk Art Center

graphic moment, perhaps to show their mothers' proficiency in the production of both.

The most vigorous of these small surfaces suggest a purposeful selection of pattern and set (See illustration 117); but others seem simply to have been drawn from already existing elements. The body of work a quiltmaker left to the next generation consisted not only of completed quilts but often of several unquilted tops, occasionally a stack of blocks that had never been worked into the whole, or in some cases a sewing basket of small pieces cut but not sewn. It is as though some sense of creative urgency pushed her to attempt a new pattern or to use a new bit of fabric before the work that last inspired her had been brought to fruition. Sometimes these other beginnings seem to have worked their way eventually into quilts for children. In some instances the quiltmaker seems to have drawn from her sewing basket a block or two originally intended for another, larger purpose and worked it, with other elements, into a quilt of smaller substance, either on the reverse (See illustration 118) or on the front.

The surface of a small Maine quilt (See illustration 119) seems to contain a number of these beginnings. Several patterns are recognizable, although each full-size block has been cut in half. The central field of the quilt consists of three panels of these strange constructions, perhaps an unfinished quilt top cut and rearranged to seem less ponderous in the smaller area. Blocks of various patterns have also been cut to form the quilt's border. A note attached to the quilt reads, "This is Grandpa R.'s cradle quilt. Aunt Lilla."

121. Third quarter nineteenth century
34³/₄ x 28¹/₂ in. (88.3 x 72.4 cm)
Private collection

No matter how imaginative the surface composition, pieced quilts for children were usually constructed of a series of identically patterned repetitive blocks. Only rarely do we see the type of sampler quilt that was worked in larger numbers for larger beds. On one of those occasional exceptions (See illustration 120) we see a sampler of blocks made small. The individual blocks it contains are examples of those more generally joined with others to form an overall design (See illustration 121), or separated by strips (See illustrations 122 and 123), or other blocks to form single units of repeated designs.

Occasionally, single geometric shapes

122. Virginia
Second quarter nineteenth century
49^1/$_2$ x 39^3/$_4$ in. (125.7 x 101 cm)
The Valentine Museum

formed the entire surface of the quilt, such as the multiple triangles that form the surface of the cradle quilt on which the merry twins and their cat are sitting (See illustration 124). In more patterned arrangements those same triangles could be sewn into strips to simulate Streaks of Lightning (See illustration 125), or worked in block units to create Pinwheels (See illustration 122) or the suggestion of Ocean Waves (See illustration 126). The geometric regularity of single squares of cotton in patterned rows of color suggested to some quiltmakers the regularity of the Philadelphia Pavement (See illustration 127) that Mrs. Trollope had observed during her 1827 journey from London to view the "domestic manners of the Americans":

123. Undated photograph
Collection of Robert Cargo Folk Art Gallery, Tuscaloosa, Alabama

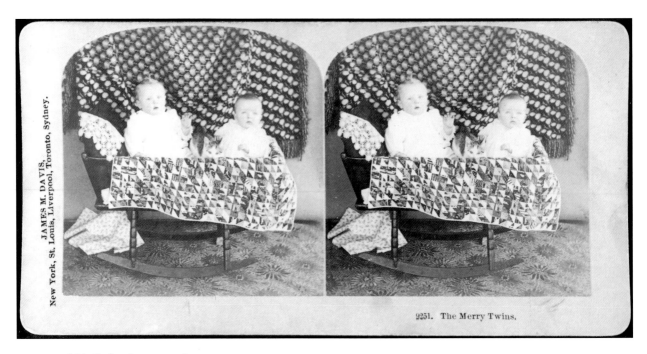

JAMES M. DAVIS,
New York, St. Louis, Liverpool, Toronto, Sydney.

9251. The Merry Twins.

124. Undated stereograph
"The Merry Twins"
Private collection

The city is built with extreme and almost wearisome regularity; the streets, which run north and south, are distinguished by numbers, from one to—I know not how many, but I paid a visit in Twelfth, street; these are intersected at right angles by others, which are known by the names of various trees.[5]

The simple square presented a delightful diversity in its use on quilts for children (See illustrations 128 and 129). For the Amish in Pennsylvania it served as the central motif for Lancaster County's classic quilted surface, where it was worked in at least one instance (See illustration 130) for a small member of that plain, devout, agrarian, and separate religious community.[6]

Even in the last quarter of the nineteenth century, quiltmakers continued to experiment with pieced shapes, and in Mennonite communities in Pennsylvania we know that children were covered with curved seams (See illustration 131), and irregular strips (See illustration 132), and cotton crazy patches (See illustration 133). But modest Four Patch (See illustration 134) blocks were the type on which young girls continued to learn how to piece America's quilt patterns, and it was the simple Nine Patch that continued in particular favor with all nineteenth-century women who set about to make a pieced quilt for a crib (See illustration 135), cradle, or trundle bed (See illustrations 136 and 137).

125. Pennsylvania
Fourth quarter nineteenth century
36 x 34 in. (91.4 x 86.4 cm)
Ex collection Marilyn and Ron Kowaleski

126. Mennonite
Pennsylvania
Fourth quarter nineteenth century
42 x 34 in. (106.7 x 86.4 cm)
Collection of Tom Cuff

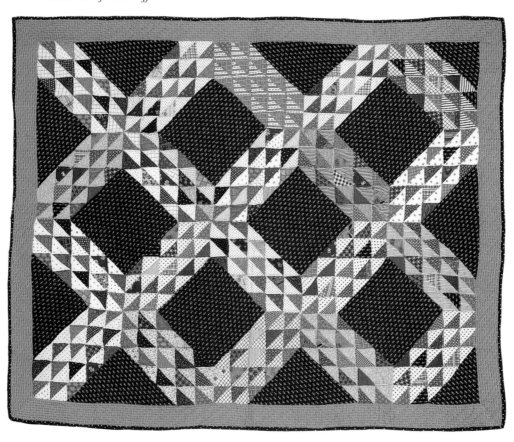

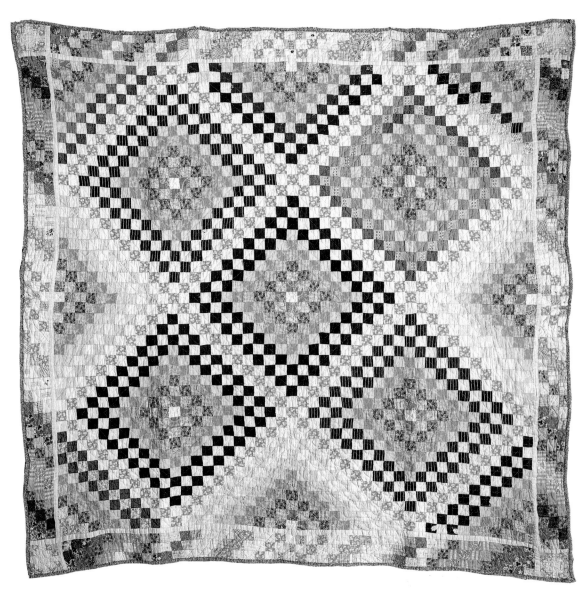

127. Fourth quarter nineteenth century
41 x 41 in. (104.1 x 104.1 cm)
The Baltimore Museum of Art, gift of Linda and
Irwin Berman, St. Simons Island, Georgia

128. Third quarter nineteenth century
36½ x 34¾ in. (92.7 x 88.3 cm)
Collection of Linda Reuther/Hearts and Hands/
San Anselmo, California

129. Third quarter nineteenth century
43 x 42 in. (109.2 x 106.7 cm)
Collection of Tom Cuff

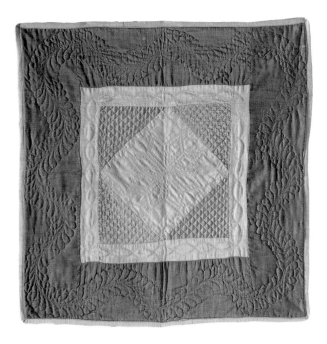

130. Amish
Lancaster County, Pennsylvania
Late nineteenth century
40 x 40 in. (101.6 x 101.6 cm)
Private collection
Photograph courtesy of America Hurrah
Antiques, NYC

131. Mennonite
Fourth quarter nineteenth century
37 x 36½ in. (94 x 92.7 cm)
Private collection
Photograph courtesy of America Hurrah
Antiques, NYC

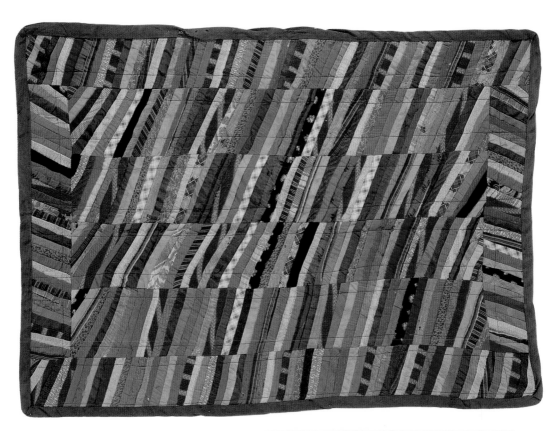

132. Mennonite
Pennsylvania
Fourth quarter nineteenth century
39 x 27^1/$_2$ in. (99.1 x 69.9 cm)
Private collection
Photograph courtesy of America Hurrah
Antiques, NYC

133. Mennonite
Pennsylvania
Late nineteenth century
54 x 41 in. (137.2 x 104.1 cm), detail
Private collection

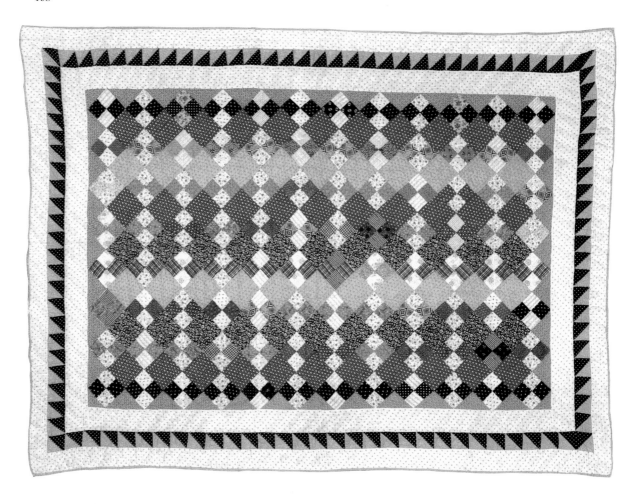

134. Dayton, Ohio
Second quarter nineteenth century
43 x 31$\frac{1}{4}$ in. (109.2 x 79.4 cm)
Collection of Freyda Rothstein

135. Ohio
Third quarter nineteenth century
34$\frac{1}{4}$ x 34$\frac{1}{4}$ in. (87 x 87 cm)
*Collection of Stella Rubin Antiques, Potomac,
Maryland*

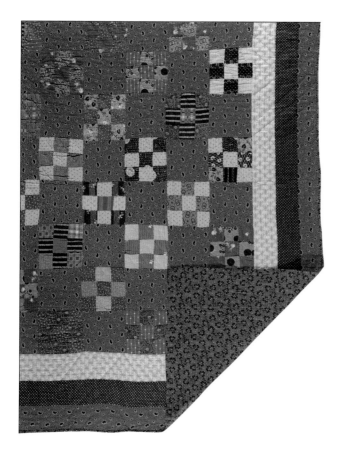

137. Frontispiece from *A Visit from St. Nicholas* (1849)
Designed and engraved by Boyd
Private collection

136. Mennonite
Pennsylvania
Fourth quarter nineteenth century
70 x 50½ in. (177.8 x 128.3 cm), detail
Private collection

NOTES

1. Jennings, 89.
2. Seegmiller, 175.
3. Ibid.
4. Ibid., 174.
5. Trollope, 210.
6. See Granick for detailed information and illustrations on Amish quilts worked in Pennsylvania and elsewhere.

138. Frontispiece from *The Well Bred Boy* (1839)
Courtesy of the Society for the Preservation of New England Antiquities

139. Handkerchief
"Sing a song of sixpence, A pocket full of rye,"
7⅝ x 11 in. (19.4 x 27.9 cm)
Collection of Mary Hunt Kahlenberg, Textile Arts, Santa Fe, New Mexico

*L*ITERARY

INFLUENCES

This "well bred boy" of 1839 (See illustration 138) might be considered as a tribute to, and the triumph of, the effort and energy of a mother who was influenced and supported by prevailing theories on the raising of children and the keeping of one's home. Even his surroundings suggest her adherence to the advice literature of the period, those innumerable manuals and periodicals that directed themselves to household management and motherhood:

> The counterpane [in this instance, what appears to be a plain color, wholecloth quilt] should never be spread up over the bolster, but turned back neatly just below this, and the upper sheet folded back over it.[1]

Dressed in the short jacket and long trousers that would eventually be adopted as proper school uniforms, our "good boy" is in stark contrast to those youthful rascals such as Tom Sawyer and Huck Finn, who flourished in the "bad-boy" books of the next half-century. He has been provided with all the accouterments of a young scholar: a large globe, quill pens, paper, ink, and his own ample bookcases filled with volumes that were often dutifully assembled according to the published recommendations of domestic advisers such as Lydia Child.

Among the books that Mrs. Child included in *The Mother's Book* (1831), were *Rhymes for the Nursery* ("A remarkably fascinating book to children.") and *Fables for the Nursery* ("Extremely entertaining to small children, and harmless in its influence"). These she considered suitable for "Children from Four to Five Years of Age."[2] She may have tolerated illustrations such as the jester and blackbirds printed in red on an early child's handkerchief (See illustration 139). However, she was careful to

140. Handkerchief

WITH BASKET FILLED, FOR GRANNY SICK
    IN BED,
RED RIDING HOOD HER NIMBLE WAY
    DOTH TREAD,
BUT THROUGH THE WOODS FOR
    FLOWERS SHE CHANCED TO STRAY
AND THUS THE CRUEL WOLF MET ON
    HER WAY.

THE WOLF SOON LEFT HER AND RAN ON
    BEFORE,
AND QUICKLY REACHED HER POOR OLD
    GRANNY'S DOOR,
THEN STEALING IN, HE OPENED WIDE
    HIS JAW,
AND GOBBLED UP POOR GRANNY IN HIS
    MAW.

WITH GRANNY'S CAP AND DRESS IN BED
    HE LAY,
RED RIDING HOOD NEXT THINKING TO
    BETRAY,
AND SO HE WOULD BUT FOR TWO
    ARCHERS BOLD,
WHO KILLED THE WOLF AND
    STRETCHED HIM DEAD AND COLD.

NOW LITTLE MAIDENS ALL SHOULD
    WARNING TAKE,
AND NEVER IN DARK WOODS STRAIGHT
    PATHS FORSAKE,
IN BRINGING JOY, TOO, EVEN WILD-
    FLOWERS FAIL,
THUS ENDS THE MORAL OF THIS
    CHRISTMAS TALE.

13 x 11¾ in. (33 x 29.9 cm)
*Collection of Mary Hunt Kahlenberg, Textile
Arts, Santa Fe, New Mexico*

point out, "I have given a pretty large list of books for quite young children, in hopes of lessening the sale of such absurd nonsense as Mother Goose, Tom Thumb, Cock Robin—and, still worse, the unnatural horrors of Blue Beard and Jack the Giant Killer."[3] It is difficult to imagine how she might have responded to the polychrome illustration of the story of Red Riding Hood printed half a century later, although the text clearly alludes to its purpose as a moral tale (See illustration 140).

Robinson Crusoe (See illustration 141) was a continuing favorite, and Mrs. Child included it as suitable for children seven or eight years of age. Describing Defoe's work as "irresistibly fascinating," she nevertheless suggested a possible alternative: "*The Child's Robinson Crusoe* (by a very religious and sensible woman), which unquestionably has a purer influence than Defoe's celebrated work; more entertaining it cannot be. Defoe's hero is a wild, reckless, ignorant adventurer; *The Child's Robinson Crusoe* is well educated in mind and heart."[4] In spite of its popularity, and Crusoe's appear-

ance on at least one full-size quilt, it was left to the Delectable Mountains (See illustration 142) of *Pilgrim's Progress* and to Sir Walter Scott's *Lady of the Lake* to inspire two of the most identifiable of America's classic quilt patterns.[5]

The Bible was, of course, the principal literary presence in most American homes; but if there were one other, until well into the second half of the nineteenth century, that book would have been, in all likelihood, John Bunyan's *Pilgrim's Progress*. Published in 1678, throughout the next two centuries this scriptural allegory was printed and read more often than any book other than the Bible. Indeed, the two were carried together into America's far western

141. Handkerchief
"While Robinson Crusoe is walking on the beach he is astonished at / discovering the print of a mans foot on the sand."
8 x 11¾ in. (20.3 x 29.9 cm)
Collection of Mary Hunt Kahlenberg, Textile Arts, Santa Fe, New Mexico

142. New Jersey
Third quarter nineteenth century
56 x 37 in. (142.2 x 94 cm)
The Baltimore Museum of Art, gift of Linda and
Irwin Berman, St. Simons Island, Georgia
Photograph courtesy of Thos. K. Woodard
American Antiques & Quilts

frontier, where a high plains mother wrote in her diary: "Taught children their SS [Sunday school] lesson and read to them from *Pilgrim's Progress,* Bible. . . ."[6] As Emma Hill and her parents made their way to the Rocky Mountains, Emma's attention to a hymnal and to *Pilgrim's Progress* was rewarded with permission to read a few romantic novels.[7]

The popularity of Bunyan's masterpiece stemmed both from content and construc-

tion. It was written by a man who earned his living with his hands for those who did the same. It was written for common people, most of whom neither owned nor read many books, and it was therefore ideally suited to the majority of the populace of a new nation. Its adventuresome simplicity seems to have made it particularly meaningful to young readers. Where diaries, journals, and remembrances of childhood contain references to literature, one is struck by how often that book is brought to mind. In Canandaigua, New York, Caroline Cowles Richards noted in her diary entry for April 1, 1853:

> Grandmother sent me up into the little chamber to-day to straighten things and get the room ready to be cleaned. I found a little book called "Child's Pilgrim Progress, Illustrated," that I had never seen before. I got as far as Giant Despair when Anna came up and said Grand-mother sent her to see what I was doing, and she went back and told her that I was sitting on the floor in the midst of books and papers and was so absorbed in "Pil-grim's Progress" that I had made none myself.[8]

Young Lucy Larcom was affected not only by its text but by its illustrations (See illustration 143). Among the "odd estrays" of her community, including a deranged preacher and a blind woman wanderer ped-dling printed rhymes, one was especially memorable:

> The one human phenomenon that filled us little ones with mortal terror was an unknown "man with a pack on his back." I do not know what we thought he would do with us, but the sight of one always sent us breathless with fright to the shel-ter of the maternal wing. I did not at all like the picture of Christian on his way to the wicket-gate in "Pilgrim's Progress," before I had read the book, because he had "a pack on his back."[9]

At some point in time a quiltmaker saw in a particular geometric arrangement of pieced cotton the suggestion of an image central to Christian's destination:

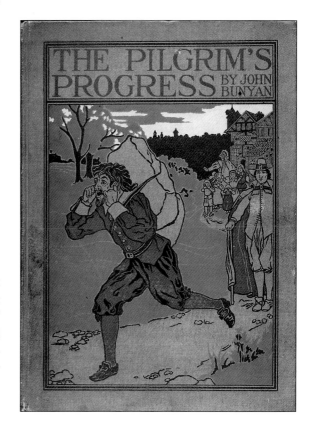

143. Book cover
The Pilgrim's Progress, by John Bunyan
(The Century Company, M DCCC XCVIII [1898])
Private collection

This small version (See illustration 144) of a particular Pennsylvania variation of Delectable Mountains was made in Bechtelsville, Berks County. The quiltmaker has worked to full scale the central field of an adult quilt and then stopped to quilt it and bind it off for a baby. A full-size quilt in a similar palette was worked in Soudertown,[11] but in sentiment the smaller quilt is perhaps more closely related to a Cumberland County quilt in this same pattern:

> The little baby's foot traced in stitching on this quilt is that of my mother's baby brother who died when he was about 3 years old (about 1853). . . . There are also the fingers of two adult hands along the border. I also see his little hand![12]

Just as we know those mountains continued to be worked on quilts for children, we know the authors of many children's books of the last half of the century reveal in their own work the continuing influence of *Pilgrim's Progress*. This is sometimes revealed through content, through characters such as John Abbott's Rollo (1858), or through a casual reference that confirms that the book was still in the popular literary vocabulary.

If Rollo and the Well Bred Boy sought to avoid the corrupting influences of questionable companions and improper behavior, there were those other popular characters who seemed to seek them out. Even Huckleberry Finn, the quintessential American boy whose education came from the experiences of life, was touched by the book:

> This table had a cover made out of beautiful oilcloth, with a red and blue spread-eagle painted on it, and a painted border

144. Bechtelsville, Berks County, Pennsylvania
Third quarter nineteenth century
35 x 35 in. (88.9 x 88.9 cm)
*Collection of Rosemarie B. and Richard S.
Machmer*
*Photograph courtesy of Thos. K. Woodard
American Antiques & Quilts*

The Delectable Mountains . . . and behold at a great distance he saw a most pleasant, Mountainous Country, beautified with Woods, Vineyards, Fruits of all sorts, Flowers also, with Springs and Fountains, very delectable to behold. . . . And when thou comest there, from hence, said they, thou mayest see to the gate of the Celestial City.[10]

all around. It come all the way from Philadelphia, they said. There was some books, too, piled up perfectly exact, on each corner of the table. One was a big family Bible full of pictures. One was *Pilgrim's Progress*, about a man that left his family, it didn't say why. I read considerable in it now and then. The statements was interesting but tough.[13]

In 1868, Louisa May Alcott published *Little Women,* and the influence of Bunyan's book is obvious and pervasive in this classic domestic novel. Chapter titles draw on Bunyan's phrases, such as "Beth Finds *The Palace Beautiful,*" "Meg Goes to *Vanity Fair,*" and "*The Valley of the Shadow.*" Instruction and conversation throughout the book are derivative, such as: "We were in the Slough of Despond tonight, and Mother came and pulled us out as Help did in the book. We ought to have our Roll of Direction, like Christian."[14] *Little Women* is more than the story of Jo and her sisters; it follows specifically the progress of four pilgrims. In the first chapter, "Playing Pilgrims," Mrs. March ("Marmee") asks:

> Do you remember how you used to play Pilgrim's Progress when you were little things? Nothing delighted you more than to have me tie my piece-bags on your backs for burdens, give you hats and sticks and rolls of paper, and let you travel through the house from the cellar, which was the City of Destruction, up, up, to the house-top, where you had all the lovely things you could collect to make a Celestial City.[15]

Beth responds: "My favorite part was when we came out on the flat roof where our flowers and arbors and pretty things were, and all stood and sung for joy up there in the sunshine."[16]

The use of quiltmaking terminology (the "piece bag") is not unique to *Little Women.* It is used throughout Alcott's work, most prominently in the closing chapter of Aunt Jo's Scrap-Bag (see Appendix).

If Bunyan's delectable mountains were meant to convey a sense of the spiritual, Scott's *The Lady of the Lake* stands as a prime example of the rise of Romanticism in the literature of the first half of the nineteenth century. A series of visual illustrations in a variety of media confirm the extraordinary popularity of Scott's 1810 poem. It was rich with imagery of the Scottish Highlands, and figurative scenes inspired by this work were frequently the subject of schoolgirl embroideries and paintings based on published prints and illustrations. A nineteenth-century watercolor (See illustration 145) and an oil on canvas (See illustration 146) both seem to be based on an engraving by David Edwin used as a frontispiece to several editions of the poem. By the middle of that century the refinements of schoolgirl academies had given way to more fundamental concepts of education, and those print-inspired embroideries had given way to a Victorian torrent of lithographed prints, and on a third related image (See illustration 147), the loose-fitting gown has yielded to contemporary fashion. Behind this newer "Lady of the Lake" float wide ribbons from a crisp-skirted, narrow-waisted dress. The contribution by American quiltmakers to this illustrative series was a fashionably rich record of the textiles from which dresses were worked, often in the immensely popular blue and white prints, and always in an interpreta-

145. Scene from *The Lady of the Lake*
     Probably 1811–25
     Watercolor, pen and ink on paper
     13⅜ x 13⁹⁄₁₆ in. (34 x 34.5 cm)
     Abby Aldrich Rockefeller Folk Art Center

146. Scene from *The Lady of the Lake*
     Oil on canvas
     23 x 25 in. (58.5 x 63.5 cm)
     Copyright ©Sotheby's, Inc.

147. Scene from *The Lady of the Lake*
Watercolor, pen and ink on paper
17¼ x 25 in. (44 x 63.5 cm)
Copyright © Sotheby's, Inc.

tion (See illustration 148) simply and sturdily their own.

As the century drew to a close, Eudotia Sturgis Wilcox worked a Storybook quilt for her granddaughter (See illustration 149) that illustrated both by fabric and by design the changes that the century had brought to American quilts and by its subject matter the great changes that had occurred in children's literature during its final decades. Cotton Mather's colonial piety (circa 1770) had yielded to the pleasure and adventure set down in Nathaniel Hawthorne's *Wonder Book for Girls and Boys* (1850). A golden period of children's literature had begun. New methods for inexpensive color reproduction, and the exceptional work of Victorian illustrators, such as Kate Greenaway and Walter Crane, resulted in a grand profusion of extraordinary images.

As with the popular illustrations from *The Lady of the Lake*, Wilcox's literary illustrations may have been drawn from specific, although as yet unidentified, sources. At least one of the small, scattered motifs can be identified (although in reverse) as the vase illustrated in an 1885 *Godey's Lady's Book*, as a "Transfer Design for Doilies in Etching" (See illustration 150). But the characters, constructed in remarkable de-

148. New York
Third quarter nineteenth century
50½ x 41½ in. (128.3 x 105.4 cm)
Ex collection Phyllis Haders

tail with considerable artistic ability, could possibly have been Eudotia's own. Three figurative vignettes illustrate the quiltmaker's ability not only with needle and thread but with paint and paintbrush, for the facial features of Heidi and her grandfather (See illustration 151), of Uncle Remus and the children who surround him (See illustration 152), and of Uncle Tom and Little

Eva (See illustration 153) have been carefully and realistically painted on the soft glove leather from which their hands and faces have been constructed.

On those endearing characters of Johanna Spyria, who introduced the Swiss Alps to the American child, the costumes are worked with great attention to construction and embellishment. The folds of Hei-

149. Full-size quilt
Made by Eudotia Sturgis Wilcox
Probably Utica, New York
Late nineteenth century
78¼ x 68 in. (198.8 x 172.7 cm)
Seaver Center for Western History Research, Los Angeles County Museum of Natural History

TRANSFER DESIGNS FOR DOILIES IN ETCHING.

150. From *Godey's Lady's Book* (July 1885)

di's skirt and sash are realistically draped, and the smallest of embroidered details have been worked on the grandfather's garments: French knots form five small buttons on each side of his knee breeches; his watch is suspended by a small metallic thread; and the sleeve of his brown velvet jacket reveals a bit of cuff.

During the years in which this quilt was assembled, American literature developed a strong interest in regionalism, as expressed in characters, mannerisms, and speech. Joel Chandler Harris's *Uncle Remus, His Songs and His Sayings: The Folk-Lore of the Old Plantation* was published in 1881 and was immensely popular during the following decade, as were other publications featuring rural characters and folktales.

To the aspects of costume and characters, Wilcox added that of social content in her illustration of Uncle Tom and Little Eva. In Brunswick, Maine, a thirty-nine-year-old mother of six had earlier written a part of this domestic southern history. Moved by the Fugitive Slave Act and inspired by a vision, Harriet Beecher Stowe sat down to write what would become the concluding chapter of a melodramatic novel that would help to alter the course of the nation. *Uncle Tom's Cabin,* published in serialized form in 1851, met with the same widespread popularity that had been accorded *Pilgrim's Progress.* Although the two were dissimilar in style (Bunyan's language was simple and direct, while Stowe wrote with a sentimentality similar to that of the Brontës), both spoke with great earnestness and conviction to the common conscience. In spite of the book's literary weaknesses, the emotional aspects of Stowe's subject

151. Detail of Illustration 149

152. Detail of Illustration 149

153. Detail of Illustration 149

were so clearly focused that sides were drawn and defined on the issues she addressed. Although *Uncle Tom's Cabin* was written for the adult, its message was wrapped in adventures grand enough to satisfy the child. In an age that strongly felt the nation to be only as good as its children, Mrs. Stowe also condensed its content for the youngest among them, and *Pictures and Stories from Uncle Tom's Cabin* was published in 1853. The preface of the small book reads: "This Little Work / Is Designed to Adapt / Mrs. Stowe's Touching Narrative / To the Understandings of the Youngest Readers / And to Foster In Their Hearts / A Generous Sympathy For The / Wronged Negro Race of America."[17]

Variations on the particular scene selected by Wilcox appeared in an 1894 edition of Stowe's book (See illustration 154) and, with twenty-four additional illustrations, on at least one child's handkerchief.[18] When

" ' Uncle Tom,' said Eva, ' I 'm going there.' "

154. From *Uncle Tom's Cabin: Or, Life Among the Lowly,* by Harriet Beecher Stowe (Houghton Mifflin, 1894)

Eudotia Wilcox worked her quilt, the Civil War had been fought and the issues that conflict addressed had been decided. Uncle Tom and the sweet blonde child were worked not in social passion but in sentimental recollection.

The geometric symmetry of those sturdy cotton Delectable Mountains was intended, perhaps, to wrap the child in a reminder of the spiritual rewards of piety and obedience; the Storybook quilt suggests the material rewards of American industry and ingenuity: silk and velvet, lace and beads, all surrounding a young girl with a confident stance, a parasol on her shoulder, and a flower in her fashionable bonnet.

NOTES

1. Herrick, 139.
2. Child, 99.
3. Ibid., 98.
4. Ibid., 102–103.
5. See Fox, *Wrapped in Glory*, 24–27, for illustration and discussion of a small figure of Robinson Crusoe, cut from an early but as yet unidentified pictorial toile, that appears on a *broderie perse* quilt in the Valentine Museum.
6. West, 169.
7. Ibid., 181.
8. Richards, 11.
9. Larcom, 35–36.
10. Bunyan, 72.
11. See Roan, 52, for illustration.
12. Lasansky, *Pieced by Mother*, 13.
13. Clemens, 143–145. See Pettit, *America's Printed and Painted Fabrics*, 137, for illustration of a painted oilcloth tablecloth seemingly identical to the one described by Huck Finn.
14. Alcott, *Little Women*, 13.
15. Ibid., 12.
16. Ibid.
17. Stowe, n.p.
18. See Weissman and Lavitt, 205, for illustration of the handkerchief in the collection of the Cooper-Hewitt Museum, Smithsonian Institution.

ANIMALS
AND PETS

There is a sweet tenderness about the small Double Hearts quilt (See illustration 155), whose central focus is a child and bird, each corner held with one small appliquéd hand. It is a quilted moment of innocence, tenderly tied to a celebration of childhood.

Just as the educational theories of Locke and Rousseau, and increasing optimism regarding infant survival, had established and encouraged new bonds of affection between parent and child, the relationship between children and animals was similarly altered. Pets were a convenient instrument of instruction through which the much-desired quality of gentleness might be instilled in the child's developing character. In 1831, *The Mother's Book* stressed that "kindness towards animals is of great importance. Children should be encouraged in pitying their distress; and if guilty of any violent treatment toward them, they

should see that you are grieved and displeased at such conduct."[1] In July 1861, *Godey's Lady's Book* advised in a somewhat more relaxed manner, "Let the little people have their live pets, by all means, even though they do give some trouble and care. Girls must have something to love, and boys something to busy themselves about." (See illustration 156)

By the middle of the century, the children themselves were their parents' pets. They were often depicted with animals by whose names they were often addressed: "Kitten" or "Bunny" or "Lamb." They were in fact often called "Pet" in their mothers' letters and their fathers' conversations and in the sentimental literature of the period. That the term was in popular use is indicated by a commercial source in the form of a laminated wood and brass doll chair bearing the pierced inscription, "PET."[2]

The child of rural America had always

155. Possibly Connecticut
Third quarter nineteenth century
38½ x 36½ in. (97.8 x 92.7 cm)
Private collection
Photograph courtesy of America Hurrah Antiques,
NYC

156. Full-size quilt
 Made by Eudotia Sturgis Wilcox
 Probably Utica, New York
 Late nineteenth century
 78¼ x 68 in. (198.8 x 172.7 cm), detail
 Seaver Center for Western History Research, Los
 Angeles County Museum of Natural History

shared its forests and fields with other creatures. Some animals were to be feared or hunted; others were to be fed, sold, or eaten, and those were often the child's responsibility within the family unit. But in the curiously intermingled aspects of their work and play, for children on the farm or frontier those same animals were frequently a source of amusement and companionship.

I was an only child, so there were no children to play with at home, only myself and cows and the dogs and the chickens.

Mother bought me dolls, tried to get me to play with them. "Pretend you're keeping house," mother said. So I took the dolls out to the shed and sat them down in chairs and tried to talk to them, but they didn't talk back. The chickens were lots more fun.[3]

This small crazy comforter (See illustration 157) would seem to have been constructed for such a farm child. The fabrics, cotton and wool, are substantial and serviceable, although they are embellished with embroidered plants and vines. The

157. New Jersey
Fourth quarter nineteenth century
39 x 39¹/₂ in. (99.1 x 100.3 cm)
The Baltimore Museum of Art, gift of Linda and
Irwin Berman, St. Simons Island, Georgia

rooster that appears on a very early child's handkerchief (See illustration 158) illustrating "the House That Jack Built" is "the Cock that crowed in the Morn that waked the Priest / all shaven and shorn that married the Man all tattered and torn / that kiffed [kissed] the Maiden all forlorn that milked the Cow with / the crumpled horn that toffed [tossed] the Dog that worried the / Cat that killed the Rat that ate the Malt that lay in the House / that Jack built." He appears beneath the maiden all forlorn who wears, coincidentally, a quilted petticoat.⁴ On this handkerchief he shares the surface with other characters, but on the crazy quilt the rooster struts alone across his multicolored barnyard.

This agrarian image was so pervasive it is impossible to point with certainty to the source that inspired this particular quiltmaker, but it is strikingly similar to other interpretations appearing on political objects and ephemera of the period. The cotton political banner (See illustration 159), for example, was hand-painted in 1880 for the campaign of a true log cabin candidate, Republican James A. Garfield, and his running mate, Chester A. Arthur. The fabrics that encircle the white embroidered rooster mirror the colors in which the Garfield rooster was painted: yellow, green, brown, orange, and orange-red.

Roosters, and other birds and animals, appeared frequently in simpler detail on children's quilts of the period, in shapes cut either freehand or with the use of patterns, such as those comprising a group of seven cut from paper feed sacks (See illustration 160).[5] The design of those less-pretentious

roosters would seem to owe more to the sharp outlines of sheet-iron weathervanes than to political symbolism.[6]

These less-detailed shapes appear on the quilt (See illustration 161) made for little Ida Euretta Cole (See illustration 162), born in 1880 in Hillsdale, Columbia County, New York. Little Ida's presence is suggested by her initials, I. E. C., those initials in fact dominating the figures of what may be her mother (Amelia) and father

158. Handkerchief
"The House That Jack Built"
10½ x 12⅜ in. (26.7 x 31.4 cm)
Collection of Mary Hunt Kahlenberg, Textile Arts, Santa Fe, New Mexico

(Michael); the similarly simple shapes of birds, cats, and dogs complete the domestic inventory.

The limited palette and the large dark shapes of a dog and a horse on this Pennsylvania crazy quilt (See illustration 163) are softened by the embroidered outlines and details by which the animals are defined, and by the smaller horse and the encircling hearts. Although it conveys in considerably less detail than does the children's alphabet handkerchief (See illustration 164) the pleasures a horse or pony could bring to childhood, it does imply the same affection.

Meta Colt Toler, whose initials appear in red cross-stitches on a reverse corner of her quilt, chose to work in a more formal style, and perhaps nowhere did an animal appear on a child's bed with greater elegance than on the splendid all-white quilt she worked in Newark, New Jersey, in the middle of the nineteenth century. A center medallion (See illustration 165) contains a small, realistically rendered, tightly stuffed horse and is surrounded by small sprays of stuffed leaves and embroidered berries. Stylistically, the horse is similar to those worked in multiple numbers across Virginia Ivey's large, all-white 1856 rendition of a fair near Russellville, Kentucky (See illustration 166).[7] Both quilts feature center medallions and quilted botanical images, and they are completed with white fringe. On each the patience and discipline required to execute the quilts seem to have been transferred to the horses themselves. Mrs. Colt's is perhaps the horse one might see pulling cart or carriage through the more fashionable sections of Newark, as *The Clinton Primer* (1830) offered up as a reward for good behavior:

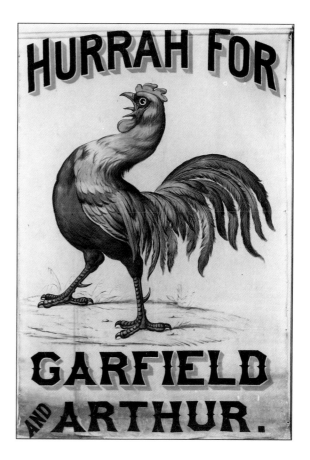

159. Political banner
Painted by Edwin Burgum, 1880
43¼ x 66¼ in. (109.9 x 168.3 cm)
New Hampshire Historical Society (#F166)

160. Paper feed bag quilt patterns
   Possibly Lancaster, Pennsylvania
   Lengths 9½ to 24 in. (24 to 61 cm)
   Copyright © Sotheby's, Inc.

The Coach and Two
Who is she that is growing up to the good fortune of riding in a coach and two? She is the girl who rises with the rising day;— whose hands and face are made clean;— whose hair is cleared of snarly locks, and neatly rolled in papers; and whose clothes are clean and whole though never gay. She who loves her book, her school, the truth and her parents, and also the path of peace and virtue.[8]

A brown and white Clamshell quilt (See illustration 167) is a quite different example of technical merit. In a curved-seam pattern, the concave and convex patches are somewhat difficult to sew, and pieced Clamshell quilts of any size are not common. In this instance, the unknown New England quiltmaker had access to a cotton fabric featuring a repeat motif of a printed horse in full gallop; and to delight the child

161. Made for Ida Euretta Cole, born October 29,
1880
Hillsdale, Columbia County, New York
Fourth quarter nineteenth century
62 x 52$\frac{1}{4}$ in. (157.5 x 132.7 cm)
Collection of Marie Michal and Peter Lubalin

162. Undated photograph of Ida Euretta Cole,
born October 29, 1880, Hillsdale, Columbia
County, New York

163. Pennsylvania
Late nineteenth century
47 x 39 in. (119.4 x 99.1 cm)
Private collection
Photograph courtesy of America Hurrah Antiques, NYC

in air, and stretches himself out in a full race. The intense energy of the beast's movement, the rush of the air, the swimming backward of lands, houses, trees, with the clattering thunder of the hoofs— all convey to the rider the fierce ecstasy which, perhaps, nothing else can give.[9]

Likewise, a young girl with the Gold Rush forty-niners wrote, "I was a fearless rider, and nothing pleased me more than to be mounted on a swift horse."[10]

Goodrich's "fierce ecstacy" applied to rider and observer alike. Horse racing in all forms was a favorite American amusement, illustrated in genre paintings and Victorian lithographs, and on copperplate toiles and roller-printed cottons. In a faded vintage photograph (See illustration 168), two children are posed before a full-size Steeple-chase, a pattern easily translated to the reduced requirements of a smaller quilt (See illustration 169) for an infant. But according to the theories of childrearing that prevailed in her period and place, the quilt-maker may have so identified that geometric pattern at some peril, for the horse race was considered a dangerous source of temptation. Another of the moral admonitions contained in *The Clinton Primer* of 1830 asked of the reader:

for whom the quilt was intended, she centered that motif in each of the alternating white clamshells. Surely this horse was the horse of every childhood dream! Samuel Goodrich recalled of his New England boyhood:

> I became a bold rider at an early age. Before I was eight years old I frequently ventured to put a horse to his speed, and that, too, without a saddle. A person who has never tried it can scarcely conceive of the wild delight of riding a swift horse, when he lays down his ears, tosses his tail

> Who loves a horse race? Are not too many fond of it? Does it not lead to many evils, and to frequent ruin? Never go to a horse race. Mr. Mix had one child, whom he called Irene; he had also a good farm, and some money. He went to the races with his child, dressed in black crepe for the loss of her Mother. Here Mr. Mix drank freely, and bet largely, and lost all he was worth. At night he went home a beggar; took a dose of brandy, and died before morning, leaving his child a penniless orphan. Never go to a horse race.[11]

164. Handkerchief
8¼ x 11½ in. (21 x 29.2 cm)
*Collection of Mary Hunt Kahlenberg, Textile
Arts, Santa Fe, New Mexico*

165. Made by Meta Colt Toler
Newark, New Jersey
60 x 35½ in. (152.4 x 90.2 cm), detail
*Collection of The Newark Museum, gift of Miss
Aimee C. Toler*

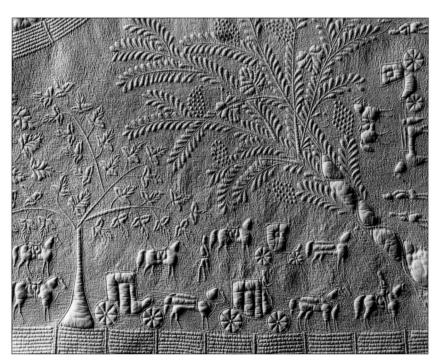

166. Made by Virginia M. Ivey
Logan County, Kentucky
Quilted inscription, "1856 A REPRESENTA-
TION OF THE FAIR NEAR RUSSELLVILLE
KENTUCKY"

95 x 98 in. (241.3 x 248.9 cm), detail
Smithsonian Institution (Photo no. 43581-D)

167. New England
Third quarter nineteenth century
31½ x 32½ in. (80 x 82.6 cm), detail
Collection of Ludy Strauss/The Quilt Gallery

168. Undated photograph
Collection of Robert Cargo Folk Art Gallery,
Tuscaloosa, Alabama

169. Ohio
Third quarter nineteenth century
31¾ x 29 in. (80.7 x 73.7 cm)
Ex collection Phyllis Haders

Other horses pranced and leaped on the sides of America's barns and fences in the lithographed posters that signaled to American children the arrival of the grandest amusement of all, the circus! In Canandaigua, New York, Caroline Cowles Richards's diary recorded:

July 4, [1857]—Barnum's circus was in town to-day and if Grandmother had not seen the pictures on the hand bills I think she would have let us go. She said it was all right to look at the creatures God had made but she did not think he ever intended that women should go only half dressed and stand up and ride on horses bare back, or jump through hoops in the air (See illustration 170). So we could not go. We saw the street parade though and heard the band play and saw the men and women in a chariot, all dressed so fine, and we saw a big elephant (See illustration 171) and a little one and a camel with an awful hump on his back, and we could hear the lion roar in the cage, as they went by. It must have been nice to see them close to and probably we will some day.[12]

As with horse races, many of the clergy, educators, and newspapermen in a still strongly puritanical environment saw the circus as one more road to moral ruination. Nevertheless, in spite of time, and of grandmothers, it continued to bring the wonders of the world to the backwoods of America. It moved by whatever means of transportation were, at that time, joining the nation together: wagons along muddy roads, "floating palace" riverboats down the Mississippi and the Ohio, and, at last, the rails.

170. Attributed to Mrs. Edwin Hardman
Fourth quarter nineteenth century
82 x 70 in. (208.3 x 177.8 cm), detail
Collection of the Haggin Museum, Stockton, California, gift of Nora LeQuellec and Marie Freeman

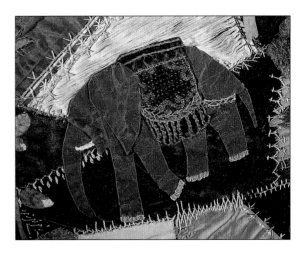

171. Full-size quilt
Made by Eudotia Sturgis Wilcox
Probably Utica, New York
Late nineteenth century
78¼ x 68 in. (198.8 x 172.7 cm), detail
Seaver Center for Western History Research, Los Angeles County Museum of Natural History

172. Possibly Maine
   Third quarter nineteenth century
   53 x 50 in. (134.6 x 127 cm)
   The Baltimore Museum of Art, gift of Linda and
   Irwin Berman, St. Simons Island, Georgia
   Photograph courtesy of Thos. K. Woodard
   American Antiques & Quilts

Surrounded by six cotton handkerchiefs illustrating other amusements,[13] the textile that comprises the center of this tied comforter (See illustration 172) is a montage of those vignettes[14] that in other printed forms drew American children to parades and circus tents and fields. The paper posters ("STUPENDOUSLY MAGNIFICENT!" "TEN THOUSAND WONDERS FROM EVERY LAND!" "THE GREATEST SHOW ON EARTH!") eventually gave way to wind and rain and sun, but the images on this cotton fabric evoke a bright and beloved memory.

NOTES

1. Child, 6–7.

2. See illustration in Heininger et al., 15. The chair was manufactured by Gardner and Company, circa 1875.

3. West, 116.

4. With very few changes in the text, this rhyme appears illustrated in a number of handkerchiefs. At least one other appears showing the maiden in a quilted petticoat (illustrated in Weissman and Lavitt, 204). Three others, printed in the middle of the nineteenth century, are illustrated in Collins, nos. 218, 219, 220.

5. The same repertoire of animals represented in the group of Pennsylvania feed sack patterns (fig. 3) were worked in plain-colored fabric on the bright printed cottons used in a full-size cotton crazy quilt made by Mrs. Samuel Glover Haskins in Granville, Vermont. See illustration in National Gallery of Art exhibition catalog, 164. On this and other similar pieces the animals are often changed only slightly by the turn of a head or the placement of a paw.

6. See illustrations in Lavitt, *Animals,* 20–21.

7. See Bowman, 54–55, for illustration and discussion.

8. Johnson, 243.

9. Speare, 16.

10. West, 105.

11. Johnson, 243.

12. Richards, 88.

13. See pages 143–44.

14. In a country with a preoccupation with horses for pleasure, sport, farming, and transportation, the equestrian performances were understandably of special interest. On the fabric, a woman leaping over a banner is performing a variation on an act developed by James Robinson in 1856. Robinson was the best-known rider of that period; he turned somersaults over a banner under which his horse galloped. Horses are seen leaping through fiery rings with a daring rider. Normally horses will panic at fire but "Liberty" horses were especially trained for this trick, although they generally performed alone. A cameo image illustrates the classic Fool in a costume originated in the commedia dell'arte, and the gladiator costume worn by the equestrian astride the two horses reminds us of the circus's beginnings in ancient Rome. Born in Europe, the circus grew up in America.

173. Plate-printed handkerchiefs
England; circa 1845
Plain-weave cotton
30 x 32½ in. (76.2 x 82.5 cm)
Gift of Mrs. William A. Hutcheson (1943-31-8)
Courtesy Cooper-Hewitt, National Museum of
Design, Smithsonian Institution/Art Resource, NY

*T*OYS,
GAMES,
AND PASTIMES

*A*s if to temper the unabashed pleasure its circus panel suggests, the border of a charming comforter (See illustration 172, "Animals and Pets") contains a typical selection of the nineteenth-century children's handkerchiefs through which a child might find the quiet amusement and moral instruction that parents were encouraged to make one and the same. Usually printed in sets (See illustration 173) to be cut apart and hemmed, they proved to be easily available diversions, and in their illustration of even the most innocent of pastimes there were important lessons to be learned. The author of *My Play Is Study* (1855), for example, would have us observe in the boy and girl blowing soap bubbles (bottom left) that "The large bubble which burst so soon resembles the man who has risen and is thrown from his height, whilst the humble citizen continues his peaceful course like the smaller bubble unaffected."[1]

Nautical themes and symbols, and the pleasures and playthings they inspired, were frequently illustrated on these small textiles, as on the handkerchief (top left), "Look at My Boat."[2] If the boat was one the boy has made himself, it was even more to be admired, for although there was an abundance of manufactured toys available for those cherished children (See illustration 174):

> There is a peculiar satisfaction in inventing things for one's self. No matter if the construction be clumsy and awkward; it employs time (which is a great object in childhood), and the pleasure the invention gives is the first impulse to ingenuity and skill. For this reason, the making of little boats . . . should not be discouraged.[3]

174. Stereograph
  "Brother John's First Christmas"
  1899 (dated)
  Private collection

Nineteenth-century America admired physical labor, and a fierce loyalty to the sea and to the life's work it might offer was evident in almost every New England village, including Lucy Larcom's Massachusetts community where, she noted:

> The sea was its nearest neighbor, and penetrated to every fireside, claiming close intimacy with every home and heart. . . . Every third man you met in the street, you might safely hail as "Ship-mate," or "Skipper," or "Captain". . . . It was hard to keep the boys from going off to sea before they were grown. No inland occupation attracted them. "Landlubber" was one of the most contemptuous epithets heard from boyish lips.[4]

It was in such a community, perhaps, that this Massachusetts quilt (See illustration 175) was made. Its blocks are pieced, appliquéd, and embroidered. The names of L. T. and F. U. Norton are inscribed, as are those of Mr. and Mrs. Thomas H. Verge, the Noyes (Fannie L., Georgie L., and Harry K.) and Isa J. Russell. Mr. and Mrs. J. R. Dellow contributed an appliquéd anchor and stars. The sextant on the block signed by Wm. Griffin was imaginatively worked on a sewing machine, and Horace M. and Anna D. Sargent signed their names above a Kate Greenaway-inspired figure with her dog, adding a date (1883) to suggest the probable year of the quilt's presentation. The most intriguing block on the quilt is surely the one signed by Eugene L. Ramsdell: varying shades of red floss, worked in fine cross-stitch, from the often-used images of a boy and girl standing with their backs to us looking out to sea, here to observe a sinking ship. Underneath this scene is written, in ink, "What are the wild waves saying, Sister?" Red and white quilts with embroidered images of children and animals were popular during the period in which this piece was done, but similarly signed presentation quilts of this size are not common. The lucky child for whom this quilt was worked must have been surrounded by a number of family members and friends, as thirty-five names appear on the twenty blocks in a variety of scripts.

The toys of the first half of the nineteenth century were specifically encouraged to be didactic in nature. Blocks gave children the opportunity to put things together and take them apart, or knock them down and reassemble them, encouraging both neatness and dexterity (See illustration 176). Mrs. Child found them appropriate even on the Sabbath: "The noisy rattle and the cart which have amused them during the week, should give place to picture-books, the kitten, little blocks, or any *quiet* amusement."[5] They remained a staple in the nursery, just as Tumbling Blocks (See illustration 177) remained a staple in most quiltmakers' repertoires of patterns throughout the century. The lid of a pine box containing a rare set of carved and turned oak building blocks (See illustration 178) made in the Harvard Shaker Community is inscribed in pencil, "Made by Henry Whitten Age 67, May 28, 1893 for Thomas Stone, Age 4. Blocks to learn by."

175. Massachusetts
1883 (dated)
63 x 50$\frac{1}{2}$ in. (160 x 128.3 cm)
Collection of Kelter-Malcé

176. Illustrating "The Castle-Builder," a poem by
Henry W. Longfellow
1867
Private collection

177. Southington, Connecticut
Third quarter nineteenth century
47 x 39¾ in. (119.4 x 101 cm), detail
Smithsonian Institution

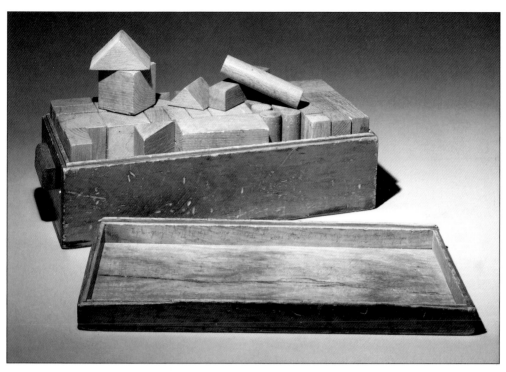

178. Pine box containing carved and turned oak building blocks, made by Henry Whitten, 1893, in the Harvard Shaker Community. Dimensions of box: height 7 in. (17.8 cm); width 22¼ in. (56.5 cm); depth 10 in. (25.4 cm)
Copyright © Sotheby's, Inc.

Games and pastimes are recorded extensively on early textiles (See illustration 179). They were extremely popular subjects for English engravings, particularly in the last quarter of the eighteenth century. The subsequent copperplate-printed textiles illustrate several games and pastimes, with children as the primary participants. Two in particular, from engravings published in 1787 and 1788 by Francesco Bartolozzi after William Hamilton's drawings, show children in five vignettes with marbles and spinning tops, and playing Bob Cherry, Hot Cockles, and Hunt the Slipper.[6] Blind Man's Buff was often shown being played by adults in plate-printed pastoral settings: one is joined with an illustration of the Judgement of Paris (circa 1790–1800), and in another (circa 1765–70) we see a woman in a quilted petticoat, pushing another in a swing.[7]

The game of Buffet the Bear, illustrated on a late-eighteenth-century handkerchief (See illustration 180), implies aspects of cruelty and humiliation that would certainly have been deemed inappropriate for "The Cheerful Companions" illustrated on the mid-nineteenth-century handkerchief (See illustration 181). Continuing as a popular subject, Blind Man's Buff appears as a frequent image on these small objects but with children as the principal players. Here the central motif is surrounded by children jumping, hopping, swinging, reading; playing at ball and with bowling hoops; and with three girls dancing.

179. Roller-printed fabric
    Alsace, France; about 1840
    Repeat height: 17 in. (43.2 cm)
    Gift of W. & J. Sloane (1943-43-28)
    Courtesy Cooper-Hewitt Museum, National
    Museum of Design, Smithsonian Institution/Art
    Resource, NY

As for dancing, within and of itself, I see no objection to it. It is a healthy, innocent, and graceful recreation. The vanity and dissipation, of which it has usually been the accompaniment, have brought it into disrepute with the conscientious. But if dancing be made to serve the purpose, which all accomplishments should serve —that of ministering to the pleasure of father, mother, brothers, sisters and friends—it is certainly innocent and becoming. I do not mean to imply that is wrong to dance anywhere else but at home. I simply mean that girls should not learn an accomplishment for the *purpose* of display among strangers.[8]

Half a century later, three young girls (probably sisters, possibly triplets) elegantly dressed even when they are jumping rope (See illustration 182), have added ribbons to their waists and dance on the surface of a crazy quilt (See illustration 183).[9]

Other quilts record the remembered pastimes of childhood in less figurative form. "When the shadows were long, and the evening breezes had cooled the earth, we little ones, whites and blacks, played Fox and Geese and Puss Wants a Corner."[10] Both games inspired pattern names: Puss in the Corner (See illustration 184) was developed in a geometric arrangement of small squares of printed cottons, and a wooden game board (See illustration 185) records another possible source for the other. A note with the carved object identifies it:

> A "game board" / made & used by New England / children. (Mansfield, Conn.) / One of the games / "Fox & Geese" / Dates in the late 1830s / Made by Wm. Chauncy Gurley Born 1823–1851 / Used by him & his sister Eliza Weed Gurley

Reading in diaries, letters, and remembrances often reveals comparative interpretations one might not have otherwise attached to these small endearments. The child's quilt (See illustration 186) worked in a variation of a pattern generally referred to as Broken Dishes, echoes the pleasure in discovering how often those bits and pieces appear in descriptions of the inventive play of young girls with no proper tiny tea sets. A young girl in West Texas placed those broken pieces in an improvised doll house furnished with a cow chip for a piano, and

180. Handkerchief
   "BUFFET the BEAR"
   Top right-hand corner: illegible inscription
   in ink, possibly "Tuphea," and below this,
   "T B W" satin-stitched in ecru silk floss
   12 x 15⅝ in. (30.5 x 39.7 cm)
   *Collection of Mary Hunt Kahlenberg, Textile
   Arts, Santa Fe, New Mexico*

181. Handkerchief
   "THE CHEERFUL COMPANIONS"
   9 x 11⅜ in. (22.9 x 28.9 cm)
   *Collection of Mary Hunt Kahlenberg, Textile
   Arts, Santa Fe, New Mexico*

182. Full-size quilt
Attributed to Mrs. Edwin Hardman
Fourth quarter nineteenth century
82 x 70 in. (208.3 x 177.8 cm), detail
Collection of the Haggin Museum, Stockton, California, gift of Nora LeQuellec and Marie Freeman

183. Another detail of Illustration 182

another "set out tables for expected guests with bits of broken china, and left our numerous rag-children tucked in asleep under mullein-blankets or plantain-coverlets."[11] Allegra Cronk's mother told her often of her girlhood home in a Canadian forest, "with the chinks between the logs for shelves in which to set her treasures of rag dolls, broken dishes, and wild flowers."[12]

For most textile and needlework scholars, the search for a print source for a design on an early needle-worked object is a fascinating academic challenge. Just as the engravings by Bartolozzi, after the drawings by Howard, can be identified on copperplate-printed textiles, engravings were also the patterns upon which many of the elegant silk schoolgirl embroideries were based.[13] Similarly, a still-unidentified print source based on the story of Palemon and Lavinia (from an eighteenth-century poem cycle, *The Seasons*, by James Thomson) was surely the source for a series of related schoolgirl needlework pieces, and for an extraordinary all-white embroidered bedcover in the Abby Aldrich Rockefeller Folk Art Center.[14]

184. Fourth quarter nineteenth century
27½ x 27½ in. (69.9 x 69.9 cm)
Ex collection Marilyn and Ron Kowaleski

185. Wooden game board, circa 1835–1840
Made by Wm. Chauncy Gurley (1823–1851)
Mansfield, Connecticut
Seaver Center for Western History Research, Los Angeles County Museum of Natural History

186. Fourth quarter nineteenth century
34¾ x 34¾ in. (88.3 x 88.3 cm)
Collection of Kelter-Malcé

187. Fourth quarter nineteenth century
37 x 35 in. (94 x 88.9 cm)
Private collection
Photograph courtesy of America Hurrah
Antiques, NYC

188. Fourth quarter nineteenth century
16 x 23 in. (40.6 x 58.4 cm), front
Shelburne Museum, Shelburne, Vermont

189. Reverse of Illustration 188

190. Stereograph
"You women are so 'fraid: she won't bleed, it's
only Vaccination."
1898 (dated)
Private collection

THE DOCTOR'S VISIT.

191. Full-size quilt
Late nineteenth century
92 x 90 in. (233.7 x 228.6 cm), detail
Laura Fisher /Antique Quilts & Americana,
NYC

To identify the print sources on figurative quilts worked later in the nineteenth century, one must often look to popular but less formal sources of illustration. Then, after the most diligent of scholarly searches, the moment of recognition can often come unexpectedly and by chance. Such is the case in one of the most endearing of all these small endearments. Scenes of Childhood (See illustration 187) was included in an exhibition, Wrapped in Glory: Figurative Quilts & Bedcovers 1700–1900, curated by the author in 1990 at the Los Angeles County Museum of Art.[15] Its related pillowcase (See illustrations 188 and 189) was later recognized as one in the collection of the Shelburne Museum, but the maker and print source for the illustrations remain unknown. For this publication, a comparative photograph had also been selected (See illustration 190) for the scene at the bottom of the quilt, "Dolly Is Sick." Then, at a casual turn of a page, a long-sought image was found. On a child's handkerchief (See illustration 191), arranged with others on the surface of a full-size quilt, was our boy/doctor, the sick dolly, and the anxious little mother! A third figure on the quilt, a girl holding a cup and spoon and standing behind the doctor, might well have appeared in the original illustration from which the design on the handkerchief was taken, if that is the order in which this vignette evolved. Coincidentally, a small handkerchief is shown in the pocket of both boys. It is a source of great joy to see these objects together, and it is hoped their publication here will lead someone, with the turning of yet another page, to discover the original printed source of this unknown quiltmaker's delight.

NOTES

1. Schorsch, 89.
2. The older boy, to whom the toy is being shown, is leaning against a large anchor and carries on his back a large bag of kelp (?). The tableaux ("Look at My Boat") invites comparison to that scene behind them in which the small figure of a man in a sou'wester is looking at the larger boat, and is thematically related to a wood engraving by Winslow Homer, "Ship Building Gloucester Harbor" (*Harper's Weekly*, Oct. 11, 1873).
3. Child, 56.
4. Larcom, 93–94.
5. Child, 67.
6. Morris, *Sports*, figs. 5, 6, 7.
7. Ibid., figs. 4, 3.
8. Child, 60–61.
9. Fox, *Wrapped in Glory*, 132–135.
10. Ward, 93.
11. West, 116; Larcom, 31.
12. Giles, 80.
13. Ring, 66–67; 74–75.
14. Fox, *Wrapped in Glory*, 42–45.
15. Ibid., 112–113.

$\mathscr{F}$OR

THE DOLLS

When a young girl begins to sew, her mother can promise her a small bed and pillow as soon as she has sewed a patch quilt for them (See illustration 192); and then a bedstead, as soon as she has sewed the sheets and cases for pillows; and then a large doll to dress, as soon as she has made undergarments; and thus go on till the whole contents of the baby-house are earned by the needle and the skill of its little owner. Thus the task of learning to sew will become a pleasure; and every new toy will be earned by useful exertion.[1]

$\mathscr{W}$riting in *The American Woman's Home* in the mid-nineteenth century, Harriet Beecher Stowe and her sister, Catherine E. Beecher, thus addressed their compatriots.

It was often through a needle and thread that American mothers transmitted to their daughters what it meant to be a woman at that time. Women occasionally taught their sons to sew, but it would more often have been as a diversion of the moment rather than as an accomplishment their daughters would carry with them the rest of their domestic lives.[2]

Throughout the nineteenth century, most American women were responsible for the sewing of their families' clothes and for their household linen. The simple stitches required for the construction of doll quilts were prerequisites to master those household responsibilities, so plain sewing began at an early age:

It was one of the earliest accomplishments of my infancy to thread my poor, half-blind Aunt Stanley's needles for her. We were close neighbors and gossips until my fourth year. Many an hour I sat by her side drawing a needle and thread through a bit of calico, under the delusion that I was sewing.

Another adopted aunt lived downstairs in the same house. This one was a sober woman; life meant business to her, and she taught me to sew in earnest, with a knot at the end of my thread, although it was only upon clothing for my rag-children—absurd creatures of my own invention, limbless and destitute of features.[3]

192. Lancaster County, Pennsylvania
    Fourth quarter nineteenth century
    6 x 7¼ in. (15.2 x 18.4 cm), pillowcase
    16 x 13½ in. (40.6 x 34.3 cm), doll quilt
    Collection of Muriel and David Greenberg
    Courtesy of Nancy Glazer

193. Maine
    Mid-nineteenth century
    7¼ x 7 in. (18.4 x 17.8 cm)
    Thelma Moore Morris Collection at Jolly Mill
    Park

194. Top: Third quarter nineteenth century
    11 x 5⅛ in. (27.9 x 13 cm)
    Private collection
    Bottom: Fourth quarter nineteenth century
    16¼ x 6 in. (41.3 x 15.2 cm)
    Private collection

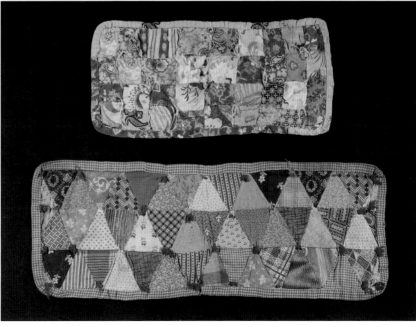

The *American Girl's Book* (1879) suggested that "children may learn to make patch-work by beginning with kettle-holders (See illustration 193), and iron-holders; and for these purposes the smallest piece of calico may be used. These holders should be lined with thick white muslin, and bound all round with tape; at one corner there should be a loop by which to hang them up."[4]

With very little additional effort or skill, the result could be a small quilt for a doll's cradle (See illustration 194), an infinitely more rewarding conclusion to those small labors. It is extremely difficult to determine which of these tiniest of quilts were worked by children, for the skill of small hands in many cases exceeded that of the large, but "we even love the irregular, coarse, ill-matched pieces, put together by a perhaps over-tasked mother, or a little child trying her first efforts at being useful."[5]

By whomever's hand it was worked, a quilt to wrap snugly around a cherished doll-child (See illustration 195) was a sweet, soft object by which a young girl might understand and perfect the role society had then assigned her. But, in her own working of such a piece (See illustration 196), she could perhaps capture for her lifetime the pure and personal pleasure of the craft.

195. Undated photograph
Courtesy of America Hurrah Antiques, NYC

What little girl does not recollect her first piece of patchwork, the anxiety for fear the pieces would not fit, the eager care with which each stitch was taken, and the delight of finding the bright squares successfully blended into the pretty pattern. Another square and another, and the work begins to look as if in time it might become a quilt; then as the little girl grows up to young ladyhood, the blushes flit across her cheek when, as she bends over her sewing, grandmamma suggests that making patchwork is a sign of matrimonial anticipations; then the mother exercising all her ingenuity to make a pretty quilt for the occupant of the cradle, until we go forward to the old grandmother, who finds patchwork the finest work her aged eyes and trembling fingers will permit her to undertake. From the home of the rich mother who finds expensive silk sewed in pretty patterns, the choicest covering for her darling, to the poor hovel, where every rag is treasured to eke out the winter quilt for the little ones, we find patchwork.[6]

For many a young girl in the nineteenth century (and in this century for the author, and perhaps for the reader as well), it was a grandmother who taught her to quilt. We know that was true for Ella Whittlesey, for the turning of a corner on her

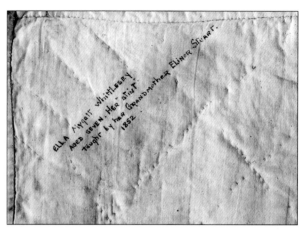

196. Maine
Fourth quarter nineteenth century
15¼ x 14 in. (38.7 x 35.6 cm)
*Thelma Moore Morris Collection at Jolly Mill
Park*

197. Detail. Inscribed in ink on the reverse of a doll
quilt:
"Ella Mygatt Whittlesey / AGED 7. Her "stint"
/ taught by her Grandmother Elinor Stuart/
1852"
*The Metropolitan Museum of Art, purchase, Mrs.
Rogers Brunschwig Gift, 1988 (1988.213.)*

Chimney Sweep doll quilt (See illustration 197) tells us so: "Ella Mygatt Whittlesey / Aged seven. Her "stint" / taught by her Grandmother Elinor Stuart. / 1852." The simple construction of a small number of four-patch (See illustration 198) or nine-patch (See illustration 199) blocks would place their successful completion well within the grasp of even a very young girl. For her beginning doll quilts, or for cradle quilts for infant brothers and sisters, it was suggested that "the outside border should be four long strips of calico, all of the same sort and not cut into patches. The dark and light calico should always be properly contrasted in arranging patch-work."[7] This would serve as a technical preparation for the more inventive construction of pieced borders (See illustration 200) and their multiple arrangements around a central field (See illustrations 201 and 202).

In addition to the charm of these small surfaces of pieced squares and triangles, and beginning with the small faux-palampore (See illustration 14, "Chintz and the Early Years"), doll quilts serve as reduced reminders of the aesthetic and technical development of their larger counterparts. The image of a crested bird (See illustration 203) that appeared on a richly glazed piece of imported fabric (circa 1825) appears (surely by chance) on a doll quilt (See illustration 204) made in Manayunk, Pennsylvania, over a half-century later. The earlier English bird poses grandly amid undulating branches and exotic flowers, while its plainer cousin perches precariously on an unyielding stalk of berries. Even that feath-

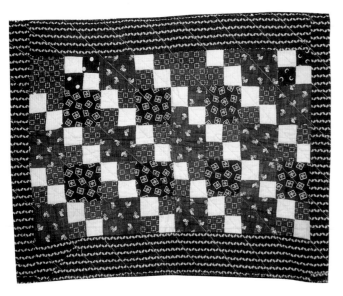

198. Indiana
Fourth quarter nineteenth century
24½ x 20 in. (62.2 x 50.8 cm)
Collection of Ardis and Robert James

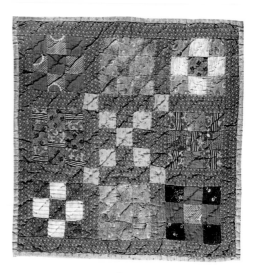

199. Lancaster, Pennsylvania
Late nineteenth century
12½ x 12¼ in. (31.8 x 31.1 cm)
Collection of Muriel and David Greenberg
Courtesy of Nancy Glazer

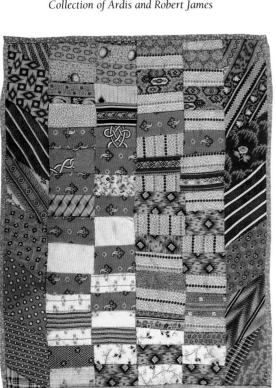

200. Fourth quarter nineteenth century
15⅞ x 12½ in. (40.3 x 31.8 cm)
Private collection

201. New England
Third quarter nineteenth century
15½ x 15½ in. (39.4 x 39.4 cm)
Collection of Glendora Hutson

202. Ohio
Third quarter nineteenth century
17½ x 14 in. (44.5 x 35.6 cm)
Collection of Muriel and David Greenberg

ered country kin—padded, as are the flowers—has been embellished with a variety of embroidered stitches.

As patterns and techniques moved easily from full-size quilts to those for small children, they were further compressed to apply to still smaller quilts. Elegant edgings have been affixed, both ruffled (See illustration 205) and fringed (See illustrations 206 and 207). In the tradition of the album quilts worked mid century in Baltimore, an appliquéd lyre (See illustration 208) and

203. Block-printed fabric
First quarter nineteenth century
Private collection

204. Manayunk, Pennsylvania
Third quarter nineteenth century
18½ x 16¾ in. (47 x 42.6 cm)
Collection of Evie Gleason

laurel leaves (See illustration 209) are drawn from the decorative arts. Small floral sprays flourish (See illustration 210), and two abbreviated blocks of Oak Leaf and Reel (See illustration 211) manage to grow on a doll-cradle quilt less than eight inches wide. Given the popularity of crazy quilts at the end of the nineteenth century, the use of that technique on doll quilts (See illustration 212) is not unexpected, but it is remarkable to find this rather obscure variation of that technique, a "tile" arrangement worked rather raggedly on sixteen uneven three-inch blocks (See illustration 213).[8]

For a quiltmaker to turn from the patchwork on those small delights to the patchwork ever present in her sewing basket must have seemed wearisome indeed, and

(Continued on page 165)

205. New England
Third quarter nineteenth century
20½ x 15¼ in. (52.1 x 38.7 cm), including ruffle
Collection of Muriel and David Greenberg
Courtesy of Nancy Glazer

206. Third quarter nineteenth century
14½ x 16¼ in. (36.8 x 41.3 cm), front including fringe
Private collection

207. Reverse of Illustration 206

208. Third quarter nineteenth century
17¼ x 17½ in. (43.8 x 44.5 cm)
Private collection

209. Allentown, Pennsylvania
Third quarter nineteenth century
23½ x 23½ in. (59.7 x 59.7 cm)
Collection of Evie Gleason

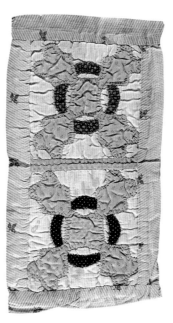

210. Third quarter nineteenth century
23 x 23 in. (58.4 x 58.4 cm)
Collection of Nancy Glazer

211. Mid-nineteenth century
13½ x 7¼ in. (34.3 x 18.4 cm)
*Collection of Muriel and David
Greenberg
Courtesy of Nancy Glazer*

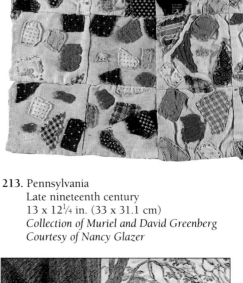

212. New England
    Fourth quarter nineteenth century
    10½ x 9 in. (26.7 x 22.9 cm)
    Collection of Muriel and David Greenberg
    Courtesy of Nancy Glazer

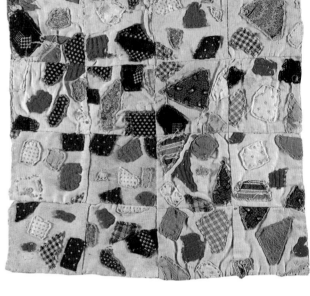

213. Pennsylvania
    Late nineteenth century
    13 x 12¼ in. (33 x 31.1 cm)
    Collection of Muriel and David Greenberg
    Courtesy of Nancy Glazer

214. Frontispiece from *Susanna and Sue* (Houghton
    Mifflin, 1909)
    Private collection

233. Third quarter nineteenth
century
14¾ x 12½ in. (37.5 x
31.8 cm)
*Thelma Moore Morris
Collection at Jolly Mill Park*

234. Fourth quarter nineteenth
century
15¼ x 12½ in. (38.7 x
31.8 cm)
*Thelma Moore Morris
Collection at Jolly Mill Park*

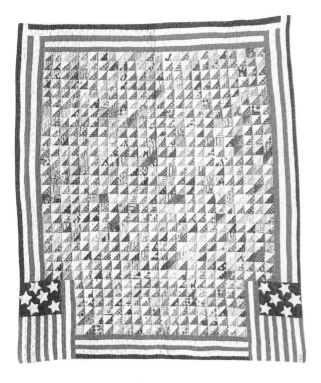

235. Pennsylvania
1862 (dated)
43½ x 36 in. (110.5 x 91.4 cm)
Private collection
Photograph courtesy of America Hurrah
Antiques, NYC

and the president ("Abe") under which he served, and the date, 1861. The 1897 obituary of Mrs. Rockhold-Teter read in part:

> She was of a family of strong, patriotic Revolutionary stock, and inherited a willingness to do and to labor that the country might grow. Her grand-father was Capt. John Rockhold, a native of Pennsylvania, who served in the War for Independence. Her father, Joseph Rockhold, moved from Pennsylvania to Ohio in 1800. He was a captain in the War of 1812. This trait of patriotism was one of the strongest in the character of Mrs. Teter. During the late war she showed her great love for the soldier boys in many ways, aiding in every way she could to encourage and help in the country's peril.[2]

If *Peterson's Magazine* can be established as the pattern source for George Teter's quilt, there is another intriguing group of patriotically inspired quilts whose printed source has yet to be determined. These quilts employ a consistent format, in which a distinctive eagle is appliquéd onto each quadrant: simplified head and neck, shield-shaped breast, widespread wings, and fanned tail (See illustration 239). The feet are generally personalized, as is the element held in the beak—a flower, cluster of cherries, leaf, cigar, firecracker, or basket. These quilts were made in considerable number, dating at least from 1876, the year of the nation's centennial celebration, and the same eagles appear in smaller but still recognizable form on a rare and well-used doll quilt (See illustration 240).

By 1840, there had been added to the flag and the eagle a third symbol capable of arousing political and patriotic fervor, that of the log cabin.

1861 edition of a popular periodical for women, *Peterson's Magazine.* The same year some Southern quiltmakers were making plans to quilt for the purchase of Confederate gunboats (See "Other Spheres"), but in Noblesville, Indiana, Mary Rockhold-Teter was inspired to reproduce the *Peterson's* pattern for her "Baby," her son George, a Union soldier (See illustration 238). She included in the quilting his name and the names of the generals (Scott and Taylor)

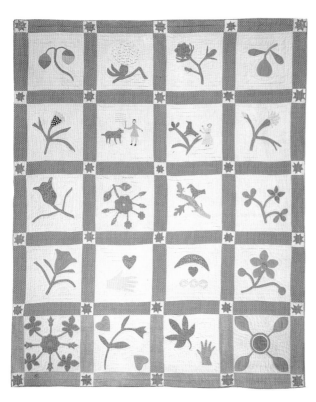

236. Made by Sarah E. Barnes (signed)
New York
Mid-nineteenth century
52 x 42 in. (132.1 x 106.7 cm)
Private collection
Photograph courtesy of America Hurrah
Antiques, NYC

237. Kansas
Third quarter nineteenth century
36⁷⁄₈ x 36³⁄₄ in. (93.7 x 93.4 cm)
From the permanent collection of the Museum of
American Folk Art, gift of Phyllis Haders

238. Made by Mary Rockhold-Teter
Noblesville, Indiana
1861 (dated)
87 x 86 in. (221 x 218.4 cm)
Smithsonian Institution (Photo no. 36635)

239. Full-size quilt
Pennsylvania
Fourth quarter nineteenth century
86 x 84³⁄₄ in. (218.4 x 215.3 cm), detail
Pilgrim/Roy Collection

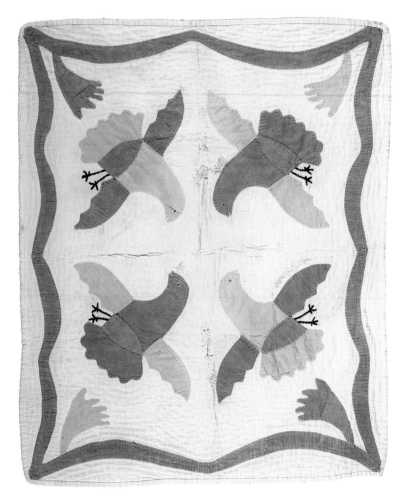

240. Fourth quarter nineteenth century
21 x 17½ in. (53.3 x 44.5 cm)
Collection of Nancy Glazer

Even before the Revolutionary War, settlers began to detach themselves from the eastern seaboard. Their first travels were along pathways in the forest, but the great river systems determined the earliest, major routes of internal migration until the French and Indian Wars opened the way for more secure expansion over land routes. Even then, the western "roads" were often only wide enough for a horse or small cart. In the first decade of the nineteenth century, there was not a major wagon road west of the Appalachians. Not until the roads were widened and improved did the great canvas-covered wagons associated with the opening of the frontier make their appearance.

There was, in fact, a succession of frontiers. For some, the trip was an elaborate undertaking. In 1816, Septima and Henry Rutledge and their five children left Charleston, South Carolina, on a six-week journey to their new plantation in Franklin County, Tennessee. Henry and his two sons rode on horseback, Septima and the three girls in a carriage and four. The entourage included more than fifty slaves, assorted livestock, and twenty wagons to carry their provisions and possessions, including Henry's extensive library and, in a separate cart, Septima's harp. They arrived at a great painted house that had been built for them.[3]

For some families on the way to the Pacific Ocean, goods and goals were more modest, and for many children the journey was often tragically incomplete:

241. Made by Eliza Dorcy Ashforth
Utah
1856
*Photograph courtesy of
Wendy Lavitt*

We had an empty cracker box which we made answer for a coffin, dug a grave in the middle of the road and deposited the dead child therein. . . . We filled the grave with stones and dirt, and when we rolled out, drove over it. Perhaps we had cheated the wolf by so doing—perhaps not.[4]

For the children who survived, there would be a splendid tale to tell, for they were a part of America's great adventure. With them went the objects and origins of America's quiltmaking tradition. In 1851, as little Adrietta Applegate and her family set out for Oregon, she was given a small bag of "quilting scraps, thread, and a thimble; she was to amuse herself along the way by learning to sew."[5] In 1856, as their wagon moved through Mill Creek Canyon, Utah, Eliza Dorcy Ashforth used threads from its cover to piece a baby dress for her daughter Sarah Ann (See illustration 241).[6]

In 1845, an editorial in the New York *Morning News* added a new phrase to the American vocabulary. It declared the country's "manifest destiny" was to "overspread and to possess the whole of the continent for the great experiment of liberty," and western expansion became a patriotic preoccupation. Even the child who remained in Virginia or Maine was intrigued by a nation moving west: the country was gripped both by the myths and by the realities.

New territories for the Western movement were quickly added: Texas in 1845, Oregon in 1846, California in 1848, and additional portions of the Southwest following the Gadsden Purchase in 1853. By 1890, when the frontier era ended, America's great dream had been realized. It was made possible in large measure by an adaptation of an architectural structure, the log cabin, introduced by Swedish settlers when they left their similarly wooded homeland to establish New Sweden in the Delaware Valley in 1638. It allowed one man with an axe to secure for himself and his family protection against the natural elements that often threatened to overwhelm even his greatest efforts.[7]

Those early settlers on the frontier, their numbers continually increasing with new immigrants and with their own growing families, became a decisive factor in national politics. Andrew Jackson, the first president to have been born in a log cabin, was swept into office by this new constituency, the common man. William Henry Harrison recognized the effective-

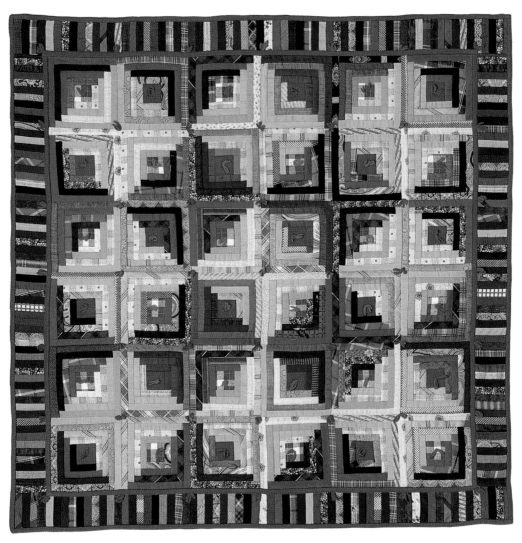

242. Pennsylvania
Fourth quarter nineteenth century
37$\frac{1}{2}$ x 37 in. (95.3 x 94 cm)
Ex collection Marilyn and Ron Kowaleski

243. From *The Bark Covered House; Or, Back in The Woods Again*, by William Nowlin (Detroit: Printed for the author, 1876)
Private collection

244. Lancaster County, Pennsylvania
Fourth quarter nineteenth century
37½ x 36¾ in. (95.3 x 93.4 cm)
Collection of Marilyn and Ron Kowaleski

245. Bucks County, Pennsylvania
Fourth quarter nineteenth century
43¼ x 34¾ in. (109.9 x 88.3 cm)
Collection of Jeannette Fink

ness of the log cabin as a political symbol and made it the theme of his 1840 campaign, even though he had been born in a fine house in Tidewater Virginia.[8] In the second half of the nineteenth century, that symbol of the common man was attached by name to a category of quilts worked in remarkable numbers.

A variety of arrangements of the small-stripped blocks from which the Log Cabin quilts were constructed resulted in a series of vigorous graphic designs that continue to suggest abstract images of the American frontier.[9] The standard Log Cabin pattern (See illustration 242) is that of four blocks turned inward and worked across the quilt, the resulting light and dark squares, on point, interlocked but visually independent. It is a suggestion of a wilderness dwelling not unlike that described by Tocqueville:

This dwelling forms as it were a little world of its own. It is an ark of civilization lost in the middle of an ocean of leaves, it is a sort of an oasis in the desert. A hundred paces beyond it is the ever-lasting forest stretching its shade around it and solitude begins again.[10]

In addition to suggesting those individual structures that provided stepping stones across the continent (See illustration 243), other small variations seemed to record the barn raisings that would bind the frontier together (See illustrations 244 and 245); in strong slashes of light and dark across the full diagonal line of the quilt, Straight Furrow (See illustrations 246, 247, and 248) may have acknowledged the pioneer dependence on each overturned row of earth; and Windmill Blades (See illustrations 249 and 250) duplicated those massive shapes seen against

246. Lancaster County, Pennsylvania
Fourth quarter nineteenth century
35³/₄ x 21 in. (90.8 x 53.3 cm)
Collection of Muriel and David Greenberg

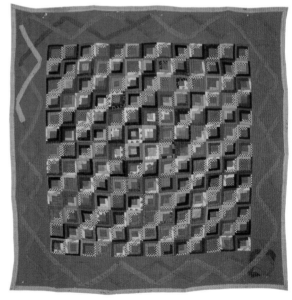

248. Mennonite
Pennsylvania
Third quarter nineteenth century
33³/₄ x 33¹/₂ in. (85.7 x 85.1 cm)
Private collection
Photograph courtesy of America Hurrah
Antiques, NYC

247. Lancaster County, Pennsylvania
Fourth quarter nineteenth century
17¹/₄ x 17¹/₈ in. (43.8 x 43.5 cm)
Collection of Muriel and David Greenberg

249. Pennsylvania
Fourth quarter nineteenth century
51 x 51 in. (129.5 x 129.5 cm)
Collection of Dr. and Mrs. Roger L. Lerner

250. Third quarter nineteenth century
46 x 46 in. (116.8 x 116.8 cm)
*The Baltimore Museum of Art, gift
of Linda and Irwin Berman,
St. Simons Island, Georgia*

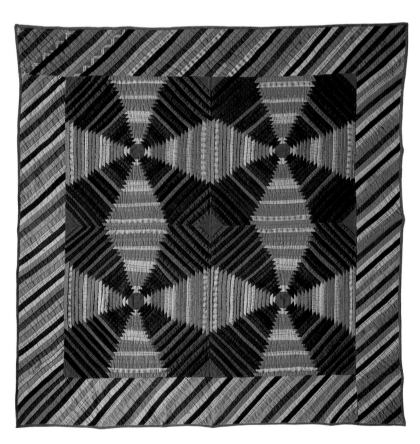

251. "The Settler's First Home in The West,"
Harper's Weekly (September 11, 1880)
Drawn by W. A. Rogers
Private collection

252. Fourth quarter nineteenth century
42³⁄₄ x 30¹⁄₄ in. (108.6 x 76.8 cm)
Private collection

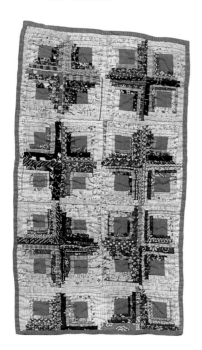

253. Pennsylvania
Fourth quarter nineteenth century
14¹⁄₂ x 8¹⁄₂ in. (36.8 x 21.6 cm)
*Thelma Moore Morris Collection at Jolly Mill
Park*

the Kansas skies where Luna Warner (See "Flying Geese") had only seen the migrating flocks.[11]

Frederick Jackson Turner wrote of the significance of the frontier in American history and of the pioneer qualities of individual initiative and self-reliance that he felt had contributed to the formation of the American character, and in what measure those qualities had been transferred to their children.[12] The settling of the West also produced many of America's most cherished myths. Perhaps American pioneers were never as good or as innocent as popular literature and the media made them out to be, but they did forge a nation and in the last half of the nineteenth century, the romantic image of the American frontier and the pioneers who settled there was what Americans perceived themselves and their country to be. The image etched in America's collective consciousness and in popular periodicals (See illustration 251) was of the log cabin, set here among endless vistas, built by the axe that leans against the open doorway; a small garden, and new chickens and piglets, and near the cattle in the background the dim image of a wagon, perhaps the one that had carried them to this distant place and these new beginnings; the father/hunter returning home to a sun-bonneted wife. Reluctant to deny what may indeed be only a magnificent myth, it is those bright barefoot children we can still imagine beneath small Log Cabin quilts, small endearments for nineteenth-century children (See illustration 252) and dolls (See illustration 253).

NOTES

1. The number nine came to have special meaning: nine states had been the first to ratify the Constitution; the first rattlesnake emblem ("Don't Tread on Me") appeared in the *Philadelphia Gazette* divided into nine sections, with the head representing all of the New England states. Mastai, 2.

2. Bowman, 57.

3. Wheeler and Neblett, 55–56.

4. Clark, 236.

5. West, 115–116.

6. Lavitt, "Children's Clothing," 31.

7. Fox, "Log Cabin," 6–13.

8. The log cabin (usually with an accompanying cider barrel) appeared on a variety of political textiles during Harrison's campaign. See Collins, 88–106, for extensive illustrations of those bandanas, banners, and broadsides.

9. It has been noted that the pattern appears on Egyptian mummies of both humans and cats, but a visual inspection of the collection of those objects in the British Museum confirms that it is a duplication of pattern line only, one achieved by multilayered "wrapping," not by the construction technique employed on quilts. Indeed, almost all geometric patterns worked on American quilts appear elsewhere in other media in other cultures. The pattern was also popular in Canada and England, illustrated in ladies' periodicals as suggestions for silk and velvet fancy work, and has continued in popularity throughout the twentieth century.

10. Tocqueville, 341.

11. For more than 40 years, from about 1863 until 1905, a massive windmill stood on the first high hill to the West of Lawrence, Kansas. Built for a milling and manufacturing business, it was an early experiment in the development of wind power that was to take place in the last part of the nineteenth century. It has been estimated that once smaller windmills became practical they were pumping water from the wells of almost every farmstead in the western two thirds of the country. Peterson, 147.

12. Turner, "Children" and *Frontier*.

254. Fourth quarter nineteenth century
26$\frac{1}{4}$ x 25$\frac{3}{4}$ in. (66.7 x 65.4 cm)
Private collection

ℰPILOGUE

On May 1, 1849, in her home on Ponus Ridge in New Canaan, Connecticut, ten-year-old Sarah Davenport began the journal that would chronicle the next three years of her young life. Within that single remarkable document she recorded a significant number of those occasions, observations, and opinions that are considered elsewhere in this book only in isolated, individual entries.

Sarah's family had not escaped the continuing realities of infant mortality. She doted on her baby brother and took on a large measure of responsibility for his care and amusement. When Burrell died at less than 16 months old, "We followed him to the grave and there his earthy remains was laid side and side with my other brother and sister and I alone remain."[1]

But for the most part, Sarah's life was one of delight and diversity. She took pleasure in their flowers ("and I am sitting on the front stoop by the side of me there is a bed of red tulips in blooming pride, a profusion of violets so modest by their side, the june roses already budding for blossoms") and pride in the garden she tended ("I walked them into the garden . . . and they had a considerable to say to us about the Asparagus.")[2]

With few exceptions, she began each entry with a comment on the weather, often noting she had gone "a huckleberrying," "a chusnuting," "a walnuting," or "a Strawberrying but had not got far before it began to Thunder and lightning and we hastened home."[3]

She played Fox and Geese, and danced to Sandy's fiddle "till we were tiard then eat some refreshment."[4] On April 17, 1850, she went to the circus in Stamford: "After we had looked at all the different animals in the cages we took our seats on one of the benches and witness some proformances by The Horse monkey and Elephant and a man that went into the lion's cage."[5]

She spent considerable time on the compositions she would submit each Wednesday to her schoolmaster, and she read consistently ("Washed a little dug Potatoes and helped prepare dinner. This afternoon Read and Wrote by turns when tired of one take the other.")[6] She read from the Bible ("I have staid at home and read the bible till amost nignt.") and from "my new book which is entitled Girls Manual,"; she read from the classics ("just before the cows came a book Pedler came along. Mother bought . . . Shakespear's works.") and from history ("have read in Hume's History of England as I do every day aloud while she [her mother] peals and cut peaches to dry occasionly I lay down my book and help her.")[7] Even at that very young age, Sarah read the newspaper ("after milking and tea read the News Pappers a little while.") and was aware of the political figures of the period ("This evening I read a part of a long Speech delivered by Mr. Clay of Kentucky, speaker in the Senate of the United States February 5 and 6th, 1850. I became interested and intend soon to read the remainder.")[8] Indeed, Sarah was to read in a copy of the *The Norwalk Gazette* a letter written by her father from the mines in California to a friend in Washington, for she was the daughter of a forty-niner who had set off to the gold fields "with the hopes of having good luck"[9] shortly after she had begun her journal. "Helped my Mother about the house work and at intervals sewed what I could because my Mother had so much sewing work to do as she is preparing cloths for Father to go to California."[10]

The work of "preparing cloths" was an ever-present activity in Sarah's life: "Our dressmaker who was engaged here, came and is to stay two or three days and I am busy plying my need in making my dresses." (Wednesday 13); "Warm and pleasant. Assisted the dressmaker" (Thursday 14); "assisted mother and the dressmaker and read aloud." (Friday 15); "Assisted my Mother and sewed in the morning" (Satur-day 16);[11] In addition to this plain sewing, "Cousin has been marking out some embroidery on silk for me to do tomorrow."[12]

Sarah's aesthetic sensibilities were strengthened by a newfound passion for pencil and paintbursh, and she began a series of the most fashionable images of the period: "I have been a drawing and painting nearly all day under Cousin Frances's guidance and the first piece is several shells with sea weeds all around it."; "I intend to have about a dozen leaves painted for an Album by the middle of next week when Cousin goes away."; "I came in and wrote one page in my writing book as I do every morning and then went to painting on my Flower and Fruit basket."[13] Were these the images she eventually brought with her plain-sewing skills to the surfaces of her quilts?

> Tuesday 20th [1852]. I have painted this forenoon and this afternoon Cousin Frances and myself have been up to Uncle Joseph's to quilt. But after we got there we found that the party was not to be untill tomorrow but however Louisa and Cornelia Scofield was there and we all quilted all the afternoon. This evening Cousin William Caroline Louisa and Cornelia came down and spent the rest of the evening and Louisa is a going to stay all night, and now Good night.[14]

NOTES

1. Davenport, 51.
2. Ibid., 28, 27.
3. Ibid., 33, 37, 37, 52.
4. Ibid., 43.
5. Ibid., 47.
6. Ibid., 57.
7. Ibid., 50, 51, 57, 61.
8. Ibid., 56, 44.
9. Ibid., 33.
10. Ibid., 33.
11. Ibid., 29.
12. Ibid., 74.
13. Ibid., 86, 88, 72.
14. Ibid., 86.

AUNT JO'S SCRAP-BAG.

MY BOYS, Etc.

By LOUISA M. ALCOTT,

AUTHOR OF "LITTLE WOMEN," "AN OLD-FASHIONED GIRL," "LITTLE MEN,"
"HOSPITAL SKETCHES."

BOSTON:

ROBERTS BROTHERS.

1872.

APPENDIX
*P*ATTY'S *P*ATCHWORK

"I perfectly hate it! and something dreadful ought to be done to the woman who invented it," said Patty, in a pet, sending a shower of gay pieces flying over the carpet as if a small whirlwind and a rainbow had got into a quarrel.

Puss did not agree with Patty, for, after a surprised hop when the flurry came, she calmly laid herself down on a red square, purring comfortably and winking her yellow eyes, as if she thanked the little girl for the bright bed that set off her white fur so prettily. This cool performance made Patty laugh more pleasantly,—

"Well, it *is* tiresome, isn't it, Aunt Pen?"

"Sometimes; but we all have to make patchwork, my dear, and do the best we can with the pieces given us."

"Do we?" and Patty opened her eyes in great astonishment at this new idea.

"Our lives are patchwork, and it depends on us a good deal how the bright and dark bits get put together so that the whole is neat, pretty, and useful when it is done," said Aunt Pen soberly.

"Deary me, now she is going to preach," thought Patty; but she rather liked Aunt Pen's preachments, for a good deal of fun got mixed up with the moralizing; and she was so good herself that children could never say in their naughty little minds, "You are just as bad as we, so you needn't talk to us, ma'am."

"I gave you that patchwork to see what you would make of it, and it is as good as a diary to me, for I can tell by the different squares how you felt when you made them," continued Aunt Pen, with a twinkle in her eye as she glanced at the many-colored bits on the carpet.

"Can you truly? just try and see," and Patty looked interested at once.

Pointing with the yard-measure, Aunt Pen said, tapping a certain dingy, puckered, brown and purple square,—

"That is a bad day; don't it look so?"

"Well, it was, I do declare! for that was the Monday piece, when every thing went wrong and I didn't care how my work looked," cried Patty, surprised at Aunt Pen's skill in reading the calico diary.

"This pretty pink and white one so neatly sewed is a good day; this funny mixture of red, blue, and yellow with the big stitches is a merry day; that one with spots on it is one that got cried over; this with the gay flowers is a day full of good little plans and resolutions; and that one made of dainty bits, all stars and dots and tiny leaves, is the one you made when you were thinking about the dear new baby there at home."

"Why, Aunt Pen, you are a fairy! How *did* you know? they truly are just as you say, as near as I can remember. I rather like that sort of patchwork," and Patty sat down upon the floor to collect, examine, and arrange her discarded work with a new interest in it.

"I see what is going on, and I have queer plays in my mind just as you little folks do. Suppose you make this a moral bed-quilt as some people make album quilts. See how much patience, perseverance, good nature, and industry you can put into it. Every bit will have a lesson or a story, and when you lie under it you will find it a real comforter," said Aunt Pen, who wanted to amuse the child and teach

"Patty's Patchwork" is from *Aunt Jo's Scrap-Bag,* by Louisa M. Alcott (Boston: Roberts Brothers, 1872).

her something better even than the good old-fashioned accomplishment of needlework.

"I don't see how I can put that sort of thing into it," answered Patty, as she gently lifted puss into her lap, instead of twitching the red bit roughly from under her.

"There goes a nice little piece of kindness this very minute," laughed Aunt Pen, pointing to the cat and the red square.

Patty laughed also, and looked pleased as she stroked Mother Bunch, while she said thoughtfully—

"I see what you mean now. I am making two kinds of patchwork at the same time; and this that I see is to remind me of the other kind that I don't see."

"Every task, no matter how small or homely, that gets well and cheerfully done, is a fine thing; and the sooner we learn to use up the dark and bright bits (the pleasures and pains, the cares and duties) into a cheerful, useful life, the sooner we become real comforters, and every one likes to cuddle about us. Don't you see, deary?"

"That's what you are, Aunt Pen;" and Patty put up her hand to hold fast by that other strong, kind, helpful hand that did so much, yet never was tired, cold, or empty.

Aunt Pen took the chubby little one in both her own, and said, smiling, yet with meaning in her eyes, as she tapped the small forefinger, rough with impatient and unskillful sewing—

"Shall we try and see what a nice little comforter we can make this month, while you wait to be called home to see mamma and the dear new baby?"

"Yes, I'd like to try;" and Patty gave Aunt Pen's hand a hearty shake, for she wanted to be good, and rather thought the new fancy would lend a charm to the task which we all find rather tiresome and hard.

So the bargain was made, and the patch Patty sewed that day was beautiful to behold; for she was in a delightfully moral state of mind, and felt quite sure that she was going to become a model for all children to follow, if they could. The next day her ardor had cooled a little, and being in a hurry to go out to play, she slighted her work, thinking no one would know. But the third day she got so angry with

her patch that she tore it in two, and declared it was all nonsense to fuss about being good and thorough and all the rest of it.

Aunt Pen did not say much, but made her mend and finish her patch and add it to the pile. After she went to bed that night Patty thought of it, and wished she could do it over, it looked so badly. But as it could not be, she had a penitent fit, and resolved to keep her temper while she sewed, at any rate, for mamma was to see the little quilt when it was done, and would want to know all about it.

Of course she did not devote herself to being good all the time, but spent her days in lessons, play, mischief, and fun, like any other lively, ten-year-older. But somehow, whenever the sewing-hour came, she remembered that talk; and as she worked she fell into the way of wondering whether Aunt Pen could guess from the patches what sort of days she had passed. She wanted to try and see, but Aunt Pen refused to read any more calico till the quilt was done: then, she said in a queer, solemn way, she should make the good and bad days appear in a remarkable manner.

This puzzled Patty very much, and she quite ached to know what the joke would be; meantime the pile grew steadily, and every day, good or bad, added to that other work called Patty's life. She did not think much about that part of it, but unconsciously the quiet sewing-time had its influence on her, and that little "conscience hour," as she sometimes called it, helped her very much.

One day she said to herself as she took up her work, "Now I'll puzzle Aunt Pen. She thinks my naughty tricks get into the patches; but I'll make this very nicely and have it gay, and then I don't see how she will ever guess what I did this morning."

Now you must know that Tweedle-dee the canary, was let out every day to fly about the room and enjoy himself. Mother Bunch never tried to catch him, though he often hopped temptingly near her. He was a droll little bird, and Patty liked to watch his promenades, for he did funny things. That day he had made her laugh by trying to fly away with a shawl, picking up the fringe with which to line the nest he was always trying to build. It was so heavy he tumbled on his back and lay kicking and pulling, but had to give it up and content himself with a bit of thread.

Patty was forbidden to chase or touch him at these times, but always felt a strong desire to have just one grab at him and see how he felt. That day, being alone in the dining-room, she found it impossible to resist; and when Tweedle-dee came tripping pertly over the table-cloth, cocking his head on one side with shrill chirps and little prancings, she caught him, and for a minute held him fast in spite of his wrathful pecking.

She put her thimble on his head, laughing to see how funny he looked, and just then he slipped out of her hand. She clutched at him, missed him, but alas, alas! he left his little tail behind him. Every feather in his blessed little tail, I do assure you; and there sat Patty with the yellow plumes in her hand and dismay in her face. Poor Tweedle-dee retired to his cage much afflicted, and sung no more that day, but Patty hid the lost tail and never said a word about it.

"Aunt Pen is so near-sighted she won't mind, and maybe he will have another tail pretty soon, or she will think he is moulting. If she asks of course I shall tell her."

Patty settled it in that way, forgetting that the slide was open and Aunt Pen was in the kitchen. So she made a neat blue and buff patch, and put it away, meaning to puzzle aunty when the reading-time came. But Patty got the worst of it, as you will see by and by.

Another day she strolled into the store-room and saw a large tray of fresh buns standing there. Now, it was against the rules to eat between meals, and new hot bread or cake was especially forbidden. Patty remembered both these things, but could not resist temptation. One plump, brown bun, with a lovely plum right in the middle, was so fascinating it was impossible to let it alone; so Patty whipped it into her pocket, ran to the garden, and hiding behind the big lilac-bush, ate it in a great hurry. It was just out of the oven, and so hot it burned her throat, and lay like a live coal in her little stomach after it was down, making her very uncomfortable for several hours.

"Why do you keep sighing?" asked Aunt Pen, as Patty sat down to her work.

"I don't feel very well."

"You have eaten something that disagrees with you. Did you eat hot biscuits for breakfast?"

"No, ma'am, I never do," and Patty gave another little gasp, for the bun lay very heavily on both stomach and conscience just then.

"A drop or two of ammonia will set you right," and Aunt Pen gave her some. It did set the stomach right, but the conscience still worried her, for she could not make up her mind to "fess" the sly, greedy thing she had done.

"Put a white patch in the middle of those green ones," said Aunt Pen, as Patty sat soberly sewing her daily square.

"Why?" asked the little girl, for aunty seldom interfered in her arrangement of the quilt.

"It will look pretty, and match the other three squares that are going at the corners of that middle piece."

"Well, I will," and Patty sewed away, wondering at this sudden interest in her work, and why Aunt Pen laughed to herself as she put away the ammonia bottle.

These are two of the naughty little things that got working into the quilt; but there were good ones also, and Aunt Pen's sharp eyes saw them all.

At the window of a house opposite Patty often saw a little girl who sat there playing with an old doll or a torn book. She never seemed to run about or go out, and Patty often wondered if she was sick, she looked so thin and sober, and was so quiet. Patty began by making faces at her for fun, but the little girl only smiled back, and nodded so good-naturedly that Patty was ashamed of herself.

"Is that girl over there poor?" she asked suddenly as she watched her one day.

"Very poor: her mother takes in sewing, and the child is lame," answered Aunt Pen, without looking up from the letter she was writing.

"Her doll is nothing but an old shawl tied round with a string, and she don't seem to have but one book. Wonder if she'd like to have me come and play with her," said Patty to herself, as she stood her own big doll in the window, and nodded back at the girl who bobbed up and down in her chair at this agreeable prospect.

"You can go and see her some day if you like," said Aunt Pen, scribbling away.

Patty said no more then, but later in the afternoon she remembered this permission, and resolved to try if aunty would find out her good doings as well as her bad ones. So, tucking Blanche Augusta Arabella Maud under one arm, her best picture-book under the other, and gathering a little nosegay of her own flowers, she slipped across the road, knocked, and marched boldly upstairs.

Mrs. Brown, the sewing-woman, was out, and no one there but Lizzie in her chair at the window, looking lonely and forlorn.

"How do you do? My name is Patty, and I live over there, and I've come to play with you," said one child in a friendly tone.

"How do you do? My name is Lizzie, and I'm very glad to see you. What a lovely doll!" returned the other child gratefully; and then the ceremony of introduction was over, and they began to play as if they had known each other for ever so long.

To poor Lizzie it seemed as if a little fairy had suddenly appeared to brighten the dismal room with flowers and smiles and pretty things; while Patty felt her pity and good-will increase as she saw Lizzie's crippled feet, and watched her thin face brighten and glow with interest and delight over book and doll and posy. "It felt good," as Patty said afterward; "sort of warm and comfortable in my heart, and I liked it ever so much." She stayed an hour, making sunshine in a shady place, and then ran home, wondering if Aunt Pen would find that out.

She found her sitting with her hands before her, and such a sad look in her face that Patty ran to her, saying anxiously,—

"What's the matter, aunty? Are you sick?"

"No, dear; but I have sorrowful news for you. Come sit in my lap and let me tell you as gently as I can."

"Mamma is dead!" cried Patty, with a look of terror in her rosy face.

"No, thank God! but the dear, new baby only stayed a week, and we shall never see her in this world."

With a cry of sorrow Patty threw herself into the arms outstretched to her, and on Aunt Pen's loving bosom sobbed away the first bitterness of her grief and disappointment.

"Oh, I wanted a little sister so much, and I was going to be so fond of her, and was so glad she came, and now I can't see or have her even for a day! I'm *so* disappointed I don't think I can bear it," sobbed Patty.

"Think of poor mamma, and bear it bravely for her sake," whispered Aunt Pen, wiping away her own and Patty's tears.

"Oh, dear me! there's the pretty quilt I was going to make for baby, and now it isn't any use, and I can't bear to finish it;" and Patty broke out afresh at the thought of so much love's labor lost.

"Mamma will love to see it, so I wouldn't give it up. Work is the best cure for sorrow; and I think you never will be sorry you tried it. Let us put a bright bit of submission with this dark trouble, and work both into your little life as patiently as we can, deary."

Patty put up her trembling lips, and kissed Aunt Pen, grateful for the tender sympathy and the helpful words. "I'll try," was all she said; and then they sat talking quietly together about the dear, dead baby, who only stayed long enough to make a place in every one's heart, and leave them aching when she went.

Patty did try to bear her first trouble bravely, and got on very well after the first day or two, except when the sewing-hour came. Then the sight of the pretty patchwork recalled the memory of the cradle it was meant to cover, and reminded her that it was empty now. Many quiet tears dropped on Patty's work; and sometimes she had to put it down and sob, for she had longed so for a little sister it was very hard to give her up, and put away all the loving plans she had made for the happy time when baby came. A great many tender little thoughts and feelings got sewed into the gay squares; and if a small stain showed here and there, I think they only added to its beauty in the eyes of those who knew what made them. Aunt Pen never suggested picking out certain puckered bits and grimy stitches, for she knew that just there the little fingers trembled, and the blue eyes got dim as they touched and saw the delicate, flowery bits left from baby's gowns.

Lizzie was full of sympathy, and came hopping over on her crutches with her only treasure, a black rabbit, to console her friend. But of all the comfort given, Mother Bunch's share was the greatest and best; for that very first sad day, as Patty wandered about the house disconsolately, puss came hurrying to meet her, and in her dumb way begged her mistress to follow and see the fine surprise prepared for her. Four plump kits as white as snow, with four gray tails all wagging in a row, as they laid on their proud mamma's downy breast, while she purred over them with her yellow eyes full of supreme content.

It was in the barn, and Patty lay for an hour with her head close to Mother Bunch, and her hands softly touching the charming little Bunches, who squeaked and tumbled and sprawled about with their dim eyes blinking, their tiny pink paws fumbling, and their dear gray tails waggling in the sweetest way. Such a comfort as they were to Patty no words could tell, and nothing will ever convince me that Mrs. Bunch did not know all about baby, and so lay herself out to cheer up her little mistress like a motherly, loving old puss, as she was.

As Patty lay on the rug that evening while Aunt Pen sung softly in the twilight, a small, white figure came pattering over the straw carpet, and dropped a soft, warm ball down by Patty's cheek, saying, as plainly as a loud, confiding purr could say it,—

"There, my dear, this is a lonely time for you, I know, so I've brought my best and prettiest darling to comfort you;" and with that Mother Bunch sat down and washed her face, while Patty cuddled little Snowdrop, and forgot to cry about baby.

Soon after this came a great happiness to Patty in the shape of a letter from mamma, saying she must have her little girl back a week earlier than they had planned.

"I'm sorry to leave you aunty, but it is so nice to be wanted, and I'm all mamma has now, you know, so I must hurry and finish my work to surprise her with. How shall we finish it off? There ought to be something regularly splendid to go all round," said Patty, in a great bustle, as she laid out her pieces, and found that only a few more were needed to complete the "moral bed-quilt."

"I must try and find something. We will put this white star, with the blue round it, in the middle, for it is the neatest and prettiest piece, in spite of the stains. I will sew in this part,

and you may finish putting the long strips together," said Aunt Pen, rummaging her bags and bundles for something fine to end off with.

"I know! I've got something!" and away hurried Lizzie, who was there, and much interested in the work.

She came hopping back again, presently, with a roll in her hand, which she proudly spread out, saying,—

"There! mother gave me that ever so long ago, but I never had any quilt to use it for, and now it's just what you want. You can't buy such chintz now-a-days, and I'm so glad I had it for you."

"It's regularly splendid!" cried Patty, in a rapture; and so it was, for the pink and white was all covered with animals, and the blue was full of birds and butterflies and bees flying about as naturally as possible. Really lovely were the little figures and the clear, soft colors, and Aunt Pen clapped her hands, while Patty hugged her friend, and declared that the quilt was perfect now.

Mrs. Brown begged to be allowed to quilt it when the patches were all nicely put together, and Patty was glad to have her, for that part of the work was beyond her skill. It did not come home till the morning Patty left, and Aunt Pen packed it up without ever unrolling it.

"We will look at it together when we show it to mamma," she said; and Patty was in such a hurry to be off that she made no objection.

A pleasant journey, a great deal of hugging and kissing, some tears and tender laments for baby, and then it was time to show the quilt, which mamma said was just what she wanted to throw over her feet as she lay on the sofa.

If there *were* any fairies, Patty would have been sure they had done something to her bed-cover, for when she proudly unrolled it, what do you think she saw?

Right in the middle of the white star, which was the centre-piece, delicately drawn with indelible ink, was a smiling little cherub, all head and wings, and under it these lines,—

"While sister dear lies asleep,
Baby careful watch will keep."

Then in each of the four gay squares that were at the corners of the strip that framed the star, was a white bit bearing other pictures and couplets that both pleased and abashed Patty as she saw and read them.

In one was seen a remarkably fine bun, with the lines,—

"Who stole the hot bun
And got burnt well?
Go ask the lilac bush,
Guess it can tell."

In the next was a plump, tailless bird, who seemed to be saying mournfully,—

"My little tail, my little tail!
This bitter loss I still bewail;
But rather ne'er have tail again
Than Patty should deceive Aunt Pen."

The third was less embarrassing, for it was a pretty bunch of flowers so daintily drawn one could almost think they smelt them, and these lines were underneath:—

"Every flower to others given,
Blossoms fair and sweet in heaven."

The fourth was a picture of a curly-haired child sewing, with some very large tears rolling down her cheeks and tumbling off her lap like marbles, while some tiny sprites were catching and flying away with them as if they were very precious:—

"Every tender drop that fell,
And Patty's sorrow lighter grew
For the gentle tears she wept."

"Oh, aunty! what does it all mean?" cried Patty, who had looked both pleased and ashamed as she glanced from one picture to the other.

"It means, dear, that the goods and bads got into the bed-quilt in spite of you, and there they are to tell their own story. The bun and the lost tail, the posy you took to poor Lizzie, and the trouble you bore so sweetly. It is just so with our lives, though we don't see it quite as clearly as this. Invisible hands paint our faults and virtues, and by and by we have to see them, so we must be careful that they are good and lovely, and we are not ashamed to let the eyes that love us best read there the history of our lives."

As Aunt Pen spoke, and Patty listened with a thoughtful face, mamma softly drew the picture coverlet over her, and whispered, as she held her little daughter close,—

"My Patty will remember this; and if all her years tell as good a story as this month, I shall not fear to read the record, and she will be in truth my little comforter."

$\mathscr{B}$IBLIOGRAPHY

Alcott, Louisa May. Aunt Jo's Scrap-Bag. Boston: Roberts Brothers, 1872.

_____. Little Women: or, Meg, Jo, Beth, and Amy. Boston: Little, Brown, 1920.

American Folk Paintings: Paintings and Drawings Other Than Portraits from the Abby Aldrich Rockefeller Folk Art Center. The Abby Aldrich Rockefeller Folk Art Center Series, edited by Beatrice T. Rumford, no. 2. Boston: Little, Brown, in Association with The Colonial Williamsburg Foundation, 1988.

Andere, Mary. Old Needlework Boxes and Tools. Newton Abbot, UK: David and Charles, 1971.

Applegate, Jesse. Recollections of My Boyhood. Roseburg, OR: Press of Review Publishing Co., 1914.

Baker, Robert H. Astronomy. Princeton, NJ: D. Van Nostrand Co., 1955.

Baumgarten, Linda R. "Dolls and Doll Clothing at Colonial Williamsburg." Antiques 140, no. 1 (1991): 102–11.

Beales, Ross W., Jr. "The Child in Seventeenth-Century America." In American Childhood: A Research Guide and Historical Handbook, edited by Joseph M. Hawes and N. Ray Hiner, 15–56. Westport, CT: Greenwood Press, 1985.

Beekman Mercantile Papers. Vol. 2. Edited by Philip L. White. New York: New York Historical Society, 1956.

Beer, Alice Baldwin. Trade Goods: A Study of Indian Chintz in the Collection of the Cooper-Hewitt Museum of Decorative Arts and Design, Smithsonian Institution. Washington, DC: Smithsonian Institution Press, 1970.

Binney, Edwin 3rd, and Gail Binney-Winslow. Homage to Amanda: Two Hundred Years of American Quilts. San Francisco: RK Press, 1984.

Bivins, John, and Forsyth Alexander. The Regional Arts of the Early South: A Sampling from the Collection of the Museum of Early Southern Decorative Arts. Winston-Salem, NC: Museum of Early Southern Decorative Arts, 1991.

"Botany for Schools." American Journal of Education (1829).

Bowman, Doris M. American Quilts: The Smithsonian Treasury. Washington, DC: Smithsonian Institution Press, 1991.

Brackman, Barbara. "What's in a Name? Quilt patterns from 1830 to the Present." In Pieced by Mother: Symposium Papers, edited by Jeannette Lasansky, 107–14. Lewisburg, PA: Oral Traditions Project of the Union County Historical Society, 1988.

Brown Eli F., Youth's Temperance Manual. New York: Van Antwerp, Bragg, 1888.

Bunyan, John. The Pilgrim's Progress. New York: Century, 1898; Pilgrim's Progress. New York: Macmillan, 1913.

Callahan, Colleen R. "A Quilt and Its Pieces." Metropolitan Museum Journal 19/20 (1986): 97–141.

Cargo, Robert. Correspondence to author, February 11, 1993.

Casteras, Susan P. Virtue Rewarded: Victorian Paintings from The Forbes Magazine Collection. Exhibition Catalog. Louisville, KY: The J. B. Speed Art Museum, 1988.

Child, Mrs. The Mother's Book. Boston: Carter and Hendee, 1831.

Clark, John H. "Overland to the Goldfields of California in 1852." Kansas Historical Quarterly 11 (1942).

Clemens, Samuel L. The Adventures of Huckleberry Finn. Cleveland: World, 1947.

Colcord, Mrs. Albert. "The Blazing Star Wanted." The National Stockman and Farmer (April 21, 1898): 18.

Collins, Herbert Ridgeway. Threads of History: Americana Recorded on Cloth 1775 to the Present. Washington, DC: Smithsonian Institution Press, 1979.

Cox, Ruth Y. Copperplate Textiles in the Williamsburg Collection: Some Sources of Design. Williamsburg, VA: Colonial Williamsburg, 1964.

D'Allemange, Henry-René. La Toile Imprimée et le Indiennes de Traite, vol. 1. Paris: Librairie Grund, 1943.

Davenport, Sarah. "The Journal of Sarah Davenport." New Canaan Historical Society Annual, 2 (1950): 26–89.

Dunton, William Rush, Jr., Old Quilts. Catonsville, MD: Published by the author, 1946.

Dye, Lee. "Pottery May Depict Massive Explosion of Star 900 Years Ago." Los Angeles Times (June 13, 1990), A3 and A18.

"Early Comets." The Essex Antiquarian 2, no. 5 (May 1898).

Ewing, Elizabeth. History of Children's Costumes. New York: Scribner, 1977.

Faill, Carol E., Curtis C. Bentzel, and Robert G. Mickey. Fraktur: A Selective Guide to the Franklin and Marshall Fraktur Collection. Lancaster, PA: Franklin and Marshall College, 1987.

Fleming, E. McClung. "Early American Decorative Arts as Social Documents." Mississippi Valley Historical Review 45, no. 2 (September 1958): 276–84.

Floud, Peter. "Copperplate Floral Designs." Antiques 71 (May 1957): 460–63.

_____. "Copperplate Pictorials." Antiques 71 (March 1957): 238–41.

_____. "The Dark-Ground Floral Chintz Style." Connoisseur 139 (May 1957): 174–78.

_____. "The Drab Style and the Designs of Daniel Goddard." Connoisseur 139 (June 1957): 234–39.

_____. English Printed Textiles 1720–1836. London: Her Majesty's Stationery Office, 1960.

_____. "Pictorial Prints of the 1820's." Antiques 72 (November 1957): 456–59.

_____. "The Pillar Print." Antiques 72 (October 1957): 352–55.

_____. "Richard Ovey and the Rise of the London 'Furniture Printers'." Connoisseur 140 (November 1957): 92–96.

Fox, Sandi. "The Log Cabin: An American Quilt on the Western Frontier," The Quilt Digest 1, (1983): 6–13.

_____. 19th Century American Patchwork Quilt. Exhibition Catalog. Tokyo: The Seibu Museum of Art, 1983.

_____. Quilts in Utah: A Reflection of the Western Experience. Exhibition Catalog. Salt Lake City: Salt Lake Art Center, 1981.

_____. Quilts: Los Angeles County Museum of Art Engagement Calendar, 1989. New York: te Neues, 1988.

_____. Small Endearments: 19th-Century Quilts for Children. New York: Scribner, 1985.

_____. Small Endearments: 19th-Century Quilts for Children and Dolls. Exhibition Catalog. Los Angeles: Municipal Art Gallery Associates, 1980.

_____. Wrapped in Glory: Figurative Quilts & Bedcovers 1700–1900. New York: Thames and Hudson/Los Angeles County Museum of Art, 1990.

Franco, Barbara. Fraternally Yours: A Decade of Collecting. Lexington, MA: Scottish Rite Masonic Museum of Our National Heritage, 1986.

_____. Masonic Symbols in American Decorative Arts. Lexington, MA: Scottish Rite Masonic Museum of Our National Heritage, 1976.

Garvan, Beatrice B., and Charles F. Hummel. The Pennsylvania Germans: A Celebration of Their Arts 1683–1850. Exhibit Catalog. Philadelphia: Philadelphia Museum of Art, 1982.

Giles, Mirandy. Tales of the Early Days. Hollywood, CA: Oxford Press, 1938.

Good Housekeeping (June 1894): 263.

Granick, Eve Wheatcroft. The Amish Quilt. Intercourse, PA: Good Books, 1989.

Hamilton, Alexander V. The Household Cyclopaedia of Practical Receipts and Daily Wants. Springfield: W. J. Holland, 1874.

Hanks, David, and Page Talbott. "Daniel Pabst: Philadelphia Cabinetmaker." Philadelphia Museum of Art Bulletin 73, no. 316 (April 1977).

Hartley, Florence. The Ladies' Hand Book of Fancy and Ornamental Work. Philadelphia: J. W. Bradley, 1861.

Hawes, Joseph M., and N. Ray Hiner, eds. American Childhood: A Research Guide and Historical Handbook. Westport, CT: Greenwood Press, 1985.

Hawthorne, Nathaniel. The Scarlet Letter. New York: Modern Library, 1950.

Heininger, Mary Lynn Stevens et al. A Century of Childhood 1820–1920. Rochester: The Margaret Woodbury Strong Museum, 1984.

Henley, Bryding Adams. "Gunboat Quilts." Alabama Heritage no. 8 (Spring 1988): 14–25.

Herrick, Christine Terhune. Housekeeping Made Easy. New York: Harper, 1888.

Hoffman, Victoria. Quilts: A Window to the Past. North Andover, MA: Museum of American Textile History, 1991.

Holmes, Kenneth L., ed. Covered Wagon Women: Diaries & Letters from the Western Trails 1840–1890, vol. 1, 1840–1849. Glendale, CA: Arthur H. Clark, 1983.

Irwin, John, and Katharine B. Brett. Origins of Chintz. London: Her Majesty's Stationery Office, 1970.

Jennings, William. "Material Progress of Utah." Utah Historical Quarterly 3, no. 3 (1930).

Johnson, Clifton. Old-Time Schools and School-books. New York: Macmillan, 1904.

Langley, Emily J. "The Patchwork Spread." Good Housekeeping (January 7, 1888): 115.

Larcom, Lucy. A New England Girlhood: Outlined from Memory. Boston: Houghton, Mifflin, 1892.

Larkin, Jack. Children Everywhere: Dimensions of Childhood in Early 19th-Century New England. Sturbridge, MA: Old Sturbridge Village, 1991.

Lasansky, Jeannette. In the Heart of Pennsylvania: 19th & 20th Century Quiltmaking Traditions. Lewisburg, PA: Oral Traditions Project of the Union County Historical Society, 1985.

_____. Pieced by Mother: Over 100 Years of Quiltmaking Traditions. Lewisburg, PA: Oral Traditions Project of the Union County Historical Society, 1987.

Lasansky, Jeannette, ed. Pieced by Mother: Symposium Papers. Lewisburg, PA: Oral Traditions Project of the Union County Historical Society, 1988.

Lavitt, Wendy. Animals in American Folk Art. New York: Knopf, 1990.

_____. "Children's Clothing on the Utah Frontier." Beehive History 15 (1989): 27–31.

Leslie, Eliza. American Girl's Book. n. p., 1879.

The Liberator (January 1, 1831); (January 2, 1837).

Lindsay, Ellen. "Patchwork." Godey's Lady's Book and Magazine (February 1857): 166–67.

Lipman, Jean. Rufus Porter Rediscovered. Exhibition Catalog. New York: The Hudson River Museum, 1980.

Longfield, Ada K. "Some Eighteenth-Century Advertisements and the English Linen and Cotton Printing Industry." Burlington Magazine 91 (March 1949): 71–73.

Low, Betty-Bright P. "Of Muslins and Merveilleuses: Excerpts from the Letters of Josephine du Pont and Margaret Manigault." Winterthur Portfolio 9, (1974): 30–75.

Mastai, Boleslaw, and Marie Louise D'Otrange. The Stars and Stripes: The Evolution of the American Flag. Fort Worth: Amon Carter Museum, 1973.

McMorris, Penny. Crazy Quilts. New York: Dutton, 1984.

Montgomery, Charles F. "A Seventeenth-Century New York Inventory." Winterthur Newsletter 8, no. 2 (February 26, 1962): 1–6; no. 3 (March 26, 1962): 1–13.

Montgomery, Florence M. Printed Textiles: English and American Cottons and Linens 1700–1850. New York: Viking, 1970.

_____. Textiles in America 1650–1870. New York: Norton, 1984.

Morris, Barbara J. "The Classical Taste in English Wood-Block Chintzes." Connoisseur 141 (April 1958): 93–97.

_____. "Copperplate Bird Designs." Antiques 71 (June 1957): 556–59.

_____. "Copperplate Chinoiseries." Antiques 71 (April 1957): 360–63.

_____. "Designs Based on Audubon's Birds of America." Antiques 72 (December 1957): 560–63.

_____. "The Indian Taste in English Wood-Block Chintzes." Connoisseur 143 (March 1959): 23-27.

_____. "Sports and Pastimes." Antiques 72 (September 1957): 252–55.

Moss, Gillian. Printed Textiles 1760–1860 in the Collection of the Cooper-Hewitt Museum. Exhibit Catalog. Washington, DC: Smithsonian Institution Press, 1987.

National Gallery of Art. An American Sampler: Folk Art from the Shelburne Museum. Exhibit Catalog. Washington, DC: National Gallery of Art, 1987.

Nowlin, William. The Bark Covered House; or, Back in The Woods Again; Being a Graphic and Thrilling Description of Real Pioneer Life in the Wilderness of Michigan. Detroit: Printed for the author, 1876.

Peck, Amelia. American Quilts & Coverlets in the Metropolitan Museum of Art. New York: Dutton/Metropolitan Museum of Art, 1990.

Peterson, John. "The Lawrence Windmill." Kansas History, vol. 3, 1980.

Pettit, Florence H. America's Indigo Blues: Resist-printed and Dyed Textiles of the Eighteenth Century. New York: Hastings House, 1974.

_____. America's Printed & Painted Fabrics 1600–1900. New York: Hastings House, 1970.

Pinckney, Eliza. The Diary of Eliza Pinckney. Edited by Harriott Horry. New York: Scribner, 1896.

Pitoiset, Gilles. Toiles Imprimées: XVIIIe-XIXe-Siécles. Paris: Société Des Amis De La Bibliothéque Forney, 1982.

Plummer, Alfred. The London Weavers' Company: 1600–1970. London: Routledge and Kegan Paul, 1972.

Richards, Caroline Cowles. Village Life in America 1852–1872: Including the Period of the American Civil War as told in The Diary of a School-Girl. Williamstown, MA: Corner House Publishers, 1972.

Ring, Betty. American Needlework Treasures: Samplers and Silk Embroideries from the collection of Betty Ring. New York: Dutton, in Association with the Museum of American Folk Art, 1987.

Roan, Nancy, and Donald Roan. Lest I Shall Be Forgotten. Green Lane, PA: Goschenhoppen Historians, 1993.

Russell, Laura. Laura Russell Remembers. Edited by Marion L. Channing. New Bedford, MA: Reynolds-Dewalt Printing, 1970.

Schlissel, Lillian, Byrd Gibbens, and Elizabeth Hampsten. Far From Home: Families of the Westward Journey. New York: Schocken Books, 1989.

Schoeser, Mary, and Celia Rufey. English and American Textiles: From 1790 to the Present. New York: Thames and Hudson, 1989.

Schorsch, Anita. Images of Childhood: An Illustrated Social History. New York: Mayflower Books, 1979.

Schulz, Constance B. "Children and Childhood in the Eighteenth Century." In American Childhood: A Research Guide and Historical Handbook, edited by Joseph M. Hawes, and N. Ray Hiner, 57–109. Westport, CT: Greenwood Press, 1985.

Seegmiller, Emma Caroll. "Personal Memories of The United Order of Orderville, Utah." Utah Historical Quarterly 7, no. 4 (1939).

Sotheby's, Inc., Sale Catalog. October 20, 1990.

Speare, Elizabeth George. Child Life in New England, 1790–1840. Sturbridge, MA: Old Sturbridge, Inc., 1961.

Spruill, Julia Cherry. Women's Life and Work in the Southern Colonies. New York: Norton, 1972.

St. Pierre, Bernardin de. The History of Paul and Virginia: or the Shipwreck. London: Printed for Ann Lemoine, 1802.

Stowe, Harriet Beecher. Pictures and Stories from Uncle Tom's Cabin. Boston: John P. Jewett, 1853.

_____. Uncle Tom's Cabin: Or, Life Among the Lowly. Boston: Houghton, Mifflin, 1894.

Tocquéville, Alexis de. Journey to America. New Haven: Yale University Press, 1960.

Trollope, Mrs. Domestic Manners of The Americans. London: Whittaker, Treacher, 1832.

Turner, Frederick Jackson. "The Children of the Pioneers." Yale Review 15 (July 1926): 645–70.

_____. The Frontier in American History. New York: Henry Holt, 1920.

Valentine, Mrs., ed. The Girl's Home Companion: A Book of Pastimes in Work and Play. New York: Frederick Warne, n.d.

Ward, Evelyn D. The Children of Bladensfield. New York: Viking, 1978.

Warner, Luna E. "The Diary of Luna E. Warner, A Kansas Teenager in the Early 1870s," edited by Venola Lewis Bivans. Kansas Historical Quarterly 35, no. 3 (Fall 1969): 276–311; no. 4 (Winter 1969): 411–41.

Weekley, Carolyn J. "Decorated Family Record Books From the Valley of Virginia." Journal of Early Southern Decorative Arts 7, no. 1 (May, 1981): 1–19.

Weissman, Judith Reiter, and Wendy Lavitt. Labors of Love: America's Textiles and Needlework, 1650–1930. New York: Knopf, 1987.

West, Elliott. Growing Up with the Country: Childhood on the Far Western Frontier. Albuquerque: University of New Mexico Press, 1989.

Wheeler, Mary Bray, and Genon Hickerson Neblett. Chosen Exile: The Life and Times of Septima Sexta Middleton Rutledge, American Cultural Pioneer. Nashville: Rutledge Hill Press, 1980.

Wiggin, Kate Douglas. Susanna and Sue. Boston: Houghton Mifflin, 1909.

Winslow, Anna Green. Diary of Anna Green Winslow: A Boston School Girl of 1771. Edited by Alice Morse Earle. Boston: Houghton, Mifflin, 1894.

$\mathcal{I}$NDEX

$\mathcal{P}$HOTOGRAPHY CREDITS

Tom Vinetz was the primary photographer for the original edition of *Small Endearments*. This revised and expanded edition required extensive additional photography, and for the excellence of those images and for his thoughtful oversight of all the photographic illustrations, I am very grateful to Steve Oliver.

The securing of images from museums, libraries, and historical societies across the country was wonderfully facilitated by curatorial staff, registrars, and photo services departments in each of the institutions listed in the Acknowledgments. In this regard I specifically acknowledge the efforts of Cathy Grosfils at the Colonial Williamsburg Foundation, Polly Mitchell at the Shelburne Museum, Bradley Nugent at the Cooper-Hewitt Museum, and Karol Schmiegel at Winterthur.

Illustrations numbers 28, 31, 35, 173, and 179 photographed by Scott Hyde; number 69 © Schecter Lee; numbers 115 (© 1989) and 197 (© 1988), © the Metropolitan Museum of Art; numbers 188 and 189 photographed by Ken Burris.